Elusive Light

A Journey Through Grief

Elusive Light

A Journey Through Grief

Mario Dell'Olio

While every precaution has been taken in the preparation of this book, the publisher assumes no responsibility for errors or omissions, or for damages resulting from the use of the information contained herein.

Cover design by Matthew David Roberts

Elusive Light
October 4, 2024.
Copyright © 2024 Mario Dell'Olio
All rights reserved. No part of this publication may be reproduced, restored in a retrieval system, or transmitted in any form or by any means, electronic, mechanical, photocopying, recording or otherwise, without the prior written permission of the author.

ISBN: 978-1-7330750-8-4

This book is memoir. It reflects the author's present recollections of experiences over time. Some names and characteristics have been changed, some events have been compressed, and some dialogue has been recreated.

To Nicoletta Di Bitetto Dell'Olio

*You nourished my creative soul
and never let me doubt my goodness or potential.
I miss you every day.*

PRAISE FOR

Elusive Light

A Journey Through Grief

An extraordinary work! Dell'Olio has crafted something magnificent. It's a treatise on grief, a memoir, a heartfelt piece in the tradition going back to the ancients of taking on life and dissecting and diagnosing and delving into it. It's a thing of wonder to be invited into another man's soul, and with this, that's precisely he's offered up to the reader.

It's written beautifully and exceptionally smart. The reader will feel that the writer here is a friend, sitting with them, talking quietly by the fire after dinner but before weariness. Dell'Olio has captured a tone of openness and conviction, somehow perfectly balanced and melded together. He's written evocatively and grippingly, with haunting descriptions and well-paced chapters. The vignettes are riveting. Most importantly, the insights are sharp. Indeed, I feel sharper for having read this. I feel graced by his wisdom. Sharing this is a gift to the world.
—Dr. Matthew Speiser, Author, Academic Dean, Historian

Award-winning author Mario Dell'Olio's memoir, "Elusive Light" is a beautifully written, openhearted chronicle of the loss of precious loved ones that brought him overwhelming grief, challenged his faith and long-held beliefs, and ultimately changed his life's journey.
—Claudia N, Oltean, Journalist, Author of Another Chance To Die

In a word, virtuosic. A raw, profound, vulnerable excavation of grief. Emotionally intimate and psychologically visceral. A powerful, unforgettable experience. Vital and stunning, a miracle in a book.
—Halo Scot, Author of Edge of the Breach

Grief by Albert Gyorgy

A Preface to Grief

by William Glenn

You may have seen the evocative sculpture by the Romanian-Swiss artist Albert Gyorgy, which sums up his life in many ways. It appears to be a bronze, outsized, and placed in a verdant landscape. It is of a Giacometti-like person with an enlarged torso—one that is hollow, empty, vacant, and visually alarming.

The sculpture is named Grief.

To see it lays you bare, empty, with a near-physical reaction, much like grief.

It is also haunting, a characteristic we often associate with profound grief—a haunting loss, incapacitating, wrenching, opaque.

And often, as well, catching us up short, not anticipating its initial fury, the bottomless vat of salty tears, the pain in the stomach, the aching in the hearts.

Who can know what we are experiencing? Who can know the depth of the pain? What words can provide comfort? When will it end, if ever? When can we breathe again?

In my life, I have encountered—how else to describe it but as an encounter—enormous grief, scalding me, searing my heart, wanting me to escape my body.

I will share one of my stories of grief as you look forward to reading Mario Dell'Olio's beautiful and wrenching account.

I worked in the AIDS epidemic for many years and buried, quite literally, many, many friends. My first impulse when the epidemic's first months arrived and our first friends were diagnosed with this deadly virus was denial and projection. I wondered why they did not just die. Knowing how crude and callous this thought was, over time, I came to understand my banal reaction as a defense, not against the virus, but against what I intuited would be years of catastrophe. Little did I know how much dying and death, and for how so very long.

But I waded into the AIDS epidemic and stayed for fifteen years, caring for the dying, holding their cancer-incrusted bodies, burying these formerly robust and beautiful young gay men, preaching at their funerals, and going back in the next day, repeating this overwhelming cycle again.

In the midst of this mass death, my mother died as well. I did not make it back in time…two hours late. Her emaciated body, mangled decades earlier by polio, was finally at rest. I preached at her funeral two days later, then got on an airplane and headed back to the AIDS epidemic.

I could not manage my grief, for, as the Irish say, not the all of it. It went where so many—especially men—bury their grief: out of sight, repressed, hidden, lurking in the belly and haunting the mind.

Several months later, I was sitting on my sofa back home, and in an instant, I grew furious. I was in a rage. I was angry at her for dying, angry at God for taking her, angry at myself for not having booked an earlier flight that fateful day, angry at not having been able to say goodbye, angry I could not kiss her one last time, angry about and towards life itself.

And I was exhausted. I had not fully grieved my friends, my beloveds Larry and David, nor so many others, not the clients I served who were also dying, not this beacon of a city, San Francisco, which was to lose 10,000 young gay men, nor the decimation of the gay community which had saved my life just a few years earlier—a young man finally bursting with joy and energy and delight and, finally in my life, hope. But that gave way.

Instead: Grief. Despair. Loneliness. Sadness. Silence.

•••

There are many reasons we grieve. As I was preparing this preface, I tallied forty-plus occasions on which we suffered significant loss. When we feel, like Gyorgy's sculpture evokes, an emptiness, a loneliness, perhaps a fear, a hollowness, sometimes a form of paralysis. And, an unspeakable silence.

Grief, notes one author, feels like a hole ripped through the fabric of your being.

We grieve the loss of our parents, of our siblings, and sometimes of our children.

We grieve the loss of dear friends, of our beloved pets, sometimes of our formerly dear marriages.

We suffer abandonment, cruelty, confusion, and we grieve that we are not able—yet—to forgive, to mend, to cauterize old wounds.

We grieve for our dear mother, the Earth.

We grieve over what might have been; we grieve the loss of our innocence, and we grieve our own self-reckoning.

We grieve.

Grief is a feeling, but more. It is a sensation in our bodies, but more. It creates cognitive confusion in its sudden presence, its bafflement, its darkness.

I sense we hold grief in our souls, that irreducible center where the most profound truths of our lives lie.

Grief is necessary, it is instructive, it is maturing.

Grief cracks open our hearts, opens us slowly to new life.

Grief binds us to our paths and imprints the love lost as a marker of the grace of our lives.

We can grieve too little, and we can grieve too long. Who knows the right amount of time for grief? Not the minds, but rather, the soul, deeper than grief, deeper than lost love, deeper than the control we have lost, not an insignificant part of grief.

Grief is, as well, a grace. Loss, death, decay are part of the great cycle of life, to which we are inextricably bound.

My friend Mario Dell'Olio has written a searing account

of grief, specifically his grief over the death of his mother, Nicoletta.

As a passionate Italian, though thoroughly American, Mario encounters a depth of grief that engulfs him and takes him to some places—spiritually, psychologically, and emotionally—that only grief has the capacity to do.

He generously describes the loss he has felt in the volume resting in your hands.

He encounters and lives through the stages of grief, like Kubler-Ross so famously—and wisely—outlined decades ago: denial, bargaining, anger, depression, and acceptance. Sometimes, it seems, Mario feels several stages at once, and some seem to barely singe him. But grieve he does, I would say, in his soul.

As his world has been deeply affected by this nearly inconsolable loss, I daresay he moves towards new life. I observe as his joy and love for his beloveds deepens, and wisdom of a new kind penetrates him. No less a personage than the late Queen of England, Elizabeth II, says, so simply: Grief is the price we pay for love.

Mario loves.

Mario is an ebullient lover: of his spouse, Jim, of his many friends, of the music that delights him and drives him professionally, of his multitude of students, of (Italian) food and entertaining. He has a joie de vivre—in an Italian translation—that emerges from his sorrow.

Your own heart will be widened by this memoir, your appreciation of the complexity of grief you bear, the everydayness and yet uniqueness of suffering, and the glimmers of hope that accompany the tears, the sadness, the emptiness and, over time, ironically, the grace that vivifies our lives to the full.

William D. Glenn, author of *I Came Here Seeking A Person,* is a psychotherapist and spiritual director, and a longtime leader in the LGBTQ+community. Influenced by Thomas Merton, Carl Jung, the Society of Jesus and Queer culture, Bill elucidates moments in his life from his childhood in an Irish Catholic family mid-20th century through his nearly decade as a Jesuit, to his subsequent life as a sober, out, married gay man. Former president of the San Francisco AIDS Foundation, executive director of Continuum HIV Services, Bill is currently the chair of the board of trustees of the Graduate Theological Union in Berkeley, an inter-religious graduate university. A co-founder of the Center for LGBTQ and Gender Studies at the Pacific School of Religion, he has focused on the intersection of queer and soul for the past four decades.

Elusive Light
A Journey Through Grief

There is a sacredness in tears. They are not the mark of weakness, but of power. They speak more eloquently than ten thousand tongues. They are the messengers of overwhelming grief, of deep contrition, and of unspeakable love.

—Washington Irving

1
THE LOSS OF LIFE

What does a person's life mean? What does it mean in the face of death? The power of death, the finality of it, causes me to question all that I've held dear—all that I've ever believed to be true. The death of a loved one is all-consuming. It is a darkness that envelopes one's entire being.

As I grieve, I feel icy water flowing through my veins and freezing around my heart. It numbs my feelings of warmth and love. Compassion and tenderness are distant, beyond my reach. In their place is emptiness, at times, filled with impatience, fear, and anger. What has crept in alongside those feelings is uncertainty. I question the idea of an afterlife—a concept I have never doubted. I do so because I don't feel the presence of those I've lost. I don't feel my beloved mother whom I loved and lost. I didn't feel her slipping away when she died. Unlike many romantic films, there was no tender moment when she came to me as she passed on to the next realm. Mom did not appear in a dream or vision to say goodbye or to tell me she loved me. The news of her death slapped me in the face and cut into my heart. Although she had been ill, the news came as a shock. I suppose we never know how we will react when that final moment comes—the moment we learn our loved one is gone. In my mother's absence, I feel a cold emptiness. If I invoke her name or call out to her, I feel no loving arms around me or stirring within my heart. Gazing into the void where her love blossomed and bore fruit, there is a vacuum. In the face of that emptiness, I realize she is gone.

My steadfast faith in God and the afterlife falters in the presence of my grief. This is a new phenomenon for me. My faith has always been a comfort to me during life's difficulties. The image of God provided solace and strength to persevere. Something has changed. It's not that I blame God for my sadness or the death of my loved ones. I know that death is part of the life cycle. It is the inevitable conclusion to everyone's earthly journey. I don't question it. However, the experience of loss leaves a hole in one's life. I feel an emptiness that cannot be filled. Memories remain painful, although some bring a bitter-sweet smile to my face. Recalling precious moments, or even the most ordinary times can be quite comforting. However, I no longer feel the presence of my mother or father. I always believed I would sense their spirit with me after they passed. I don't, and it is why my belief in the existence of an afterlife has faltered. Have I deluded myself throughout my life? Is talk of Heaven simply a means of giving comfort to the grieving? Are teachings regarding Hell just a deterrent from choosing evil actions? In our grief, there is a longing for eternal life. We desperately need to believe that those who have passed before us are "in a better place." The idea that death is final, that there is nothing beyond it, is crushing. Yet, it may very well be the reality of our existence. The very thought of this leaves me cold.

How does one make sense of the senseless? Is there a way to find meaning in an experience that crushes your very soul? Is there any point in the search for greater meaning, or is it that our defense mechanisms have kicked in and are trying to make us feel better? I have grappled with these questions for years. When I examine the various trials life has presented me with, I am struck by the enormity of suffering in the human condition. I consider myself a happy person who has led a productive and fulfilling life. Please God, I hope for many more years with those whom I love.

What prompted this reflection is the recent death of my mother. The death of a parent is a passage most of us experience. I don't claim that my grief is any more profound than anyone else's. Given the close bond we had, I knew I would struggle with the loss of a woman who loomed large in my world. During the final eighteen months of her life, I experienced what I can only call anticipatory grief. She suffered from a fractured neck and congestive heart failure among other ailments a ninety-one-year-old person might have.

We had numerous conversations about her life and the fact that she was ready to be reunited with my father, who had died thirteen years before. She shared so much with me and I with her during those months. I truly believe there was nothing left unsaid. Mom lived a long, beautiful life filled with so much love. I couldn't ask for a more peaceful understanding of her passing. However, nothing prepared me for the emptiness I feel or for the gaping hole in my heart.

I always assumed that I would feel her spirit pass on at the moment of her death. Because of our intimate bond, I believed that she would speak to me and that I would feel her presence after her death. One of my most painful realizations is that I feel nothing but loss. I don't feel her guiding spirit or her and my father looking down upon us. Instead, I feel emptiness. The void is filled with pain. This has raised some essential questions regarding what I believe. As a result, it has prompted an examination of some of the most difficult experiences in my life. In the sixth decade of my life, I find myself reliving painful moments from my late teens and twenties. My perspective and interpretation of loss and trauma have evolved, and I don't understand things the same way as when I was twenty years old. My belief in God and my spiritual journey are far from the simple faith I experienced decades ago. The meaning I drew from my struggles takes on a different hue after six decades of living. I find myself wondering if what I believed then is true. Did I have it all wrong? Do I have it wrong now?

The only way for me to understand the dark night of the soul is to revisit that darkness in search of light, a light that is elusive at this moment. As I reflect upon my journey and the pivotal experiences that formed the man I have come to be, I am struck by the number of trials I have encountered. Looking back over the decades, I realize that each event gave me new insight. Most times, that insight came many years afterward. The process of healing revealed the psychological and emotional work that was necessary in order for me to move forward. Through each journey into pain and loss, my faith in God changed, my worldview expanded, and my capacity to endure increased. One could say I grew stronger, although that is a relative term. I believe I simply grew—grew into the person I am today.

The following pages are not meant to be a "how to" manual for those experiencing loss. I don't profess to have the final word regarding the most healthy way to grieve. In fact, my recent loss revealed my inadequacy in the face of grief. It has cut me to the core and reduced me to my most simple, elemental self. I stand before a mirror stripped of honors and external validation from others. Gone are my professional and personal accomplishments. What remains as I gaze upon my reflection is my naked heart. It bears the scars of each battle with love and loss. My heart is not adorned with fancy clothing or titles. In my reflection, it beats with a steady thump telling me I'm still here despite my pain.

My hope is that my reflections give the reader insight into their own journey. Perhaps the examination of loss will provide insight or shed light on the darkness that exists in each of our lives.

HOW TO GRIEVE

The death of my mother stopped me in my tracks. My drive to move forward in my career and social life all but disappeared. Her death has prompted myriad questions. In my grief, I have begun to reflect on various events throughout my life. Images of myself as a young man trying to make sense of death and loss appear in vivid detail. Revisiting these experiences of trauma or loss raises the question of whether I ever fully dealt with or sorted through my feelings of loss. Did I truly grieve as I should have? Perhaps those aren't the right questions. I find myself examining devastating moments that occurred decades ago. I am searching for something I might have missed—looking for meaning in my struggle. I wonder if more than sixty years of life have given me a new or different perspective on death. I wonder if my life experiences allow me to glean new insights into myself concerning each loss—concerning all those I love.

I don't have the same religious zeal as I did when I was twenty years-old. My worldview has changed or evolved since my days as a young seminarian studying to be a Catholic priest.

I know that fact alone changes how I interpret the losses I've experienced. I find the need to delve into each event with new eyes, eyes that are necessarily colored by the many years that have passed. My grief has changed. The understanding or interpretation of each event is viewed from the perspective of a man in the last quarter of his life. For me, that bears examination and reflection.

The chapters that follow describe pivotal events in my life, turning points that changed the course of my life's journey. Each has transformed the person I was before. Innocence was lost at each turn, and a new pathway was forged. Like clay on a potter's wheel, I was shaped and molded into an entirely different work of art. Made from earth, the clay bears the scars of life with imperfections that give the finished product its unique beauty. Each imperfection is a map that tells the story of our lives and loves. Perhaps my journey can give insight into your losses or struggles.

Elusive Light 25

When I think of death, and of late the idea has come with alarming frequency, I seem at peace with the idea that a day will dawn when I no longer be among those living
    in this valley of strange humors.
    I can accept the idea of my own demise, but I am unable to accept the death of anyone else.
    I find it impossible to let a friend
    or relative go into that country to no return.
    Disbelief becomes my close companion,
    and anger follows in its wake.
    I answer the heroic question 'Death, where is thy sting?' with 'It is here in my heart and mind and memories.'

— Maya Angelou, When I Think of Death

2
THREE AT ONCE

There were several impactful events that changed the carefree and fun-loving boy into a deeply reflective man. My first encounter with tragic death occurred at the age of nineteen. I was unprepared for the senseless nature of what happened and the enormity of its impact on me and my family.

A college junior, I lived in an ideal setting. What used to be rows of summer beach cottages for local residents became several miles of housing for upperclassmen at Fairfield University. There were a few bars in which students gathered and a shuttle bus that ferried us back and forth to the main campus. We beach residents had our own community. Walking along the shore in the off-season revealed hidden beauty: crisp autumn days, snow blanketing the sandy beaches, and brilliant spring sunshine as vegetation sprang to life with new vigor. Lantern Point boasted a row of homes that jutted out into Long Island Sound. I lived in the most idyllic setting.

My life at Fairfield University, a Jesuit school in Connecticut, was full and happy. The Jesuits are a teaching order of priests that are often described as the intellectuals of the Church. The Latin motto is Ad majórem Dei glóriam, AMDG. From the moment we stepped onto the university campus as freshmen, we were instilled with the idea that all we did was to be for the greater glory of God. I took the motto seriously and hoped to live up to the Jesuit standards. I had a solid community of friends and was involved in many clubs and activities. I helped lead the folk group at Mass each Sunday. I was a Eucharistic minister and active in the Campus Ministry department. I was a soloist in the Glee Club and the a cappella group, which traveled throughout the spring semester giving concerts at numerous colleges and universities. My college experience was rich and fulfilling. My outlook brimmed with possibility and a bright future. Out of nowhere, the earth upon which I stood began to shake.

One morning, I was milling around our beach house preparing for my morning class when a knock startled me from my routine. Father Moy appeared at the door and I looked at him with confusion. What in the world is he doing here?

"Good morning, Mario."

"Father Moy, hi. I'm just about to go to class. What's going on? Why are you here?"

"Let's sit for a moment. I have some unpleasant news to share."

He walked into the living room and took a seat. I was eager to know why he came to my house. He hesitated as he took his time getting started.

"Please, Frank. Tell me what's going on."

"I'm sorry, Mario. I wanted to tell you in person. It's not news you should hear through a phone call. Your Aunt Lily,

Uncle John, and Uncle Nick passed away last night. They were found this morning."

"What? That's impossible. What do you mean, found? All three of them? Was it a car accident?"

I could barely breathe. My mind was racing with questions. This can't be happening. I popped up from my chair and paced the room, shooting questions at Father Moy.

Asphyxiated in their own home, they never knew what hit them. They fell asleep in place, doing ordinary tasks—my aunt at the stove cooking, one uncle at the kitchen table reading the newspaper, the other on the living room couch watching television. Their car was left running in the garage pouring carbon monoxide into the house.

Frank reached out and steadied me. Saying nothing, he pulled me into him and hugged me firmly. After a few moments, he told me to pack a few things.

"I will bring you home. You are in no condition to drive."

"But I'll need my car. I can't leave it here."

"You can figure that out later. For now, I need to get you home to your parents. They are eager to see you."

The scene at home was surreal. My three siblings and parents moved around the house in a catatonic state. Very little was said. None of us could believe what had happened. Every now and again one of us would pose a question: "How could this have happened?" "Did Uncle John get distracted when he got out of the car?" "Didn't they realize they were getting sleepy?"

I was most concerned about my cousin, Father Frank. He lost his parents and grandfather all at once. Frank and I were extremely close. We were family; we were friends. I was in the seminary program for the Diocese of Bridgeport, and Frank was my most trusted mentor. The other priests at the rectory contacted me on his behalf to ask if I would read at the funeral

Mass. Although it would be difficult, I resolved to do anything Frank asked of me. He had always been there for me and guided me through so much of my life. I wanted to show him how much he meant to me, especially in the face of this unthinkable tragedy.

The day of the funeral arrived after a grueling week. The funeral was held at St. Thomas Aquinas Church in Fairfield, Connecticut. Frank was pastor of the parish and he, along with scores of priests, presided at the funeral Mass. The wake had been overwhelming. Hundreds of people attended. The Dell'Olio family was well-established in Fairfield County. Attendees from the family alone would have filled the church. In addition, Father Frank was a beloved pastor with a heroic reputation for service in the diocese. So many parishioners, past and present, flooded through the doors to show their support. His brother priests numbered in the hundreds. The line of people waiting to pay their respects extended out the door and down the block. We expected the funeral to be standing room only.

On the morning of the funeral, we gathered at the church doors, taking our place behind three coffins. Our entire family processed into the church in a catatonic state as the organ pipes moaned and echoed throughout the sacred space. The grand church was overflowing with mourners. Once set in place, the three coffins blocked the aisle to the sanctuary. It was an ominous sight.

Father Frank moved in a trance as the Mass for his parents and grandfather progressed. I remember thinking, How is he keeping it together? It was more than anyone could ask of a person. I knew him in a way that few of my family did. Our bond went beyond friend and family member. In my formation toward the priesthood, Fr. Frank was my closest spiritual counselor. I ached for this man who I had only known as a pillar of strength—my wisdom figure. When it came time for my reading, I made my way toward the ambo, weaving my way through the coffins. As I climbed the stairs to the sanctuary, I glanced at Father Frank—we made eye contact for the briefest of moments. It was all either of us could handle. I couldn't bear seeing his all-consuming pain. He was my rock. I never knew him to be so vulnerable, so helpless.

I stood looking out at the hundreds of eyes staring up at me—stone-faced, tear-stained, sobbing faces gazed at me. I took a deep breath and began.

"A reading from the Book of Wisdom. The souls of the just are in the hand of God, and no torment shall touch them. They seemed, in the view of the foolish, to be dead; and their passing away was thought an affliction and their going forth from us, utter destruction. But they are in peace."

Those powerful words rang throughout the church. I proclaimed the faith instilled in me by my mother and father, nurtured through mentors like Frank, and challenged through my religious studies at Fairfield University. I spoke with the strength that my family needed. I became the minister of the word the gathering of mourners required. It steeled my faith as I struggled to make sense of an unfathomable tragedy. All of us moved through the grand liturgy without the need to concentrate on the prayers. We knew the ritual by heart. It was the only thing that made sense during an experience that made no sense at all. The scores of priests, the bishop, and the public in attendance created a dramatic scene. It felt as if we were watching an event on television or in a movie, except that it was so very real, and we were the mourners.

During the weeks that followed, I watched as Fr. Frank drifted further and further from me. He wasn't fully present in any conversation. His mind and broken heart were miles away.

It was the first time I had experienced someone else's grief. It was all-consuming and dark. The wall of sadness was impenetrable. Although I experienced the loss, it was nowhere as proximate or intimate for me. It was difficult to be with him during those days. The selfish part of me wanted him to move beyond his grief quickly so I could have my friend and mentor back. I wished he could be back to normal and that we could simply spend time together. That was not to be—normal did not exist, not any longer.

Even so many years later, I can never truly understand the profound loss he experienced. Grief is one's own. Nobody lives it in the exact same way. The loss of three family members at once weighed heavily on all of us, but most heavily upon Frank. Because of my relationship with him, I ignored my own sense of loss. The family mourned together during those days following their tragic deaths. But I had a grave belief that my grief paled in comparison to Frank's. Therefore, my pain was selfish or self-indulgent. Rather than talk it through and process the unimaginable circumstances of their death, I pushed it away and focused my energies on my dear cousin.

I believe many of us view the acknowledgment of our pain as feeling sorry for ourselves. We are taught to pull ourselves up from our bootstraps and get on with life. But there is a difference between wallowing in sorrow and validating it and processing it. Acknowledging the hurt allows one to address it and heal it. Denying its existence or declaring it invalid prevents us from examining how the pain affects our lives. That pain will manifest itself nonetheless in other forms such as depression, sadness, or physical ailments.

The image of three coffins filling the sanctuary of the church remains a dark memory. I could hardly fathom the untimely death of my aunt and uncles. That they all died at once in a senseless accident punctuated the loss. My optimism waned as I saw my life through darker lenses. The reality of loss has a way of coloring all that comes after it. A shadow obscured the brilliance of the sun. It darkened the vision of my future.

Grief can destroy you — or focus you. You can decide a relationship was all for nothing if it had to end in death, and you alone. OR you can realize that every moment of it had more meaning than you dared to recognize at the time, so much meaning it scared you, so you just lived, just took for granted the love and laughter of each day, and didn't allow yourself to consider the sacredness of it.

—Dean Koontz

3
FATEFUL NIGHT

The following autumn, just six months later, my life would change course once again. I was only twenty years old and I faced the most devastating moment of my brief life.

The late October chill seeped into my bones along with the cold drizzle dripping from my hair. I hurried to my car without a hat or umbrella. My discomfort did little to dampen my spirit. I was still on a high from the concert. The Pablo Cruz band performed live in the gym at Fairfield University and my ears were still ringing from the high decibel level. My friends and I were seated at the side of the stage, directly in front of the speakers. We had to shout to be heard, and then only barely so. But we were ecstatic as we danced and sang along with the band. My senior year was off to an exciting start as I looked with optimism to the holiday season just weeks away.

My new Pontiac Sunbird was parked a good distance from Alumni Hall. I ran through the parking lot, dodging the raindrops as best I could. When I finally got to it, I smiled.

Wet leaves clung to the shiny black hood that glowed from the streetlamp above. It was my first car, and although it was used, it was my pride and joy. With tan faux leather and a sporty stick shift, I felt cool in the driver's seat. I had purchased it just a couple of months before from Fr. Chuck, a priest at St. Thomas Church where my cousin was pastor. The church was less than a mile from the university. I admired Fr. Chuck for his macho look and studied detachment from all things emotional. He was the total opposite of me who reveled in the passionate expression of my beliefs and heartfelt emotions. In my mind, he was the ideal of masculine strength. As a young gay man who was not out, I viewed his hyper-masculinity as something to strive toward. I believed it was a goal out of reach. I admired his manly behavior. Buying his car gave me a vicarious feeling of participating in his macho image. Driving my Sunbird, I felt connected to that classic male persona—something I believed was lacking in my personality. Just coming to terms with my sexuality, I bore a great deal of internalized homophobia.

Once at my car, I fiddled with the key until it found its mark. The car door slammed with a solid thud and I was grateful to be out of the weather. As I pulled out of the parking lot, the rain became heavier. Sheets of water cascaded across the windshield making it difficult to see. But I knew the roads like I knew my own body. I had driven to and from campus hundreds of times. Making the decision to commute to school after two years of living on campus baffled my friends. Why would I want to go back home after experiencing the independence of campus life? But that was the trade-off for buying a car. I couldn't afford both and I desperately wanted that Sunbird. I didn't regret my decision. I loved my car and the freedom it afforded me.

My mind was filled with images of the concert and dancing along with the music as I drove through town. I had the music blaring on my radio and sang along. The car in front of me slowed to a crawl in the rain. My impatience grew with each passing block, driving at a snail's pace. What's wrong with this guy? Has he never driven in the rain? I was frustrated, wanting to get home to bed. It was already past one o'clock in the morning and it had been a long week.

Stopped at a traffic light, I pulled up beside him, relieved that I could finally get in front of him. When the light turned from red to green, I pressed the gas pedal to the floor and felt the power of my Sunbird propel me forward. I was easily a car's distance ahead of him in seconds. I eased up on the pedal and turned up the music as I settled back to a reasonable speed singing along with the music on the radio. Soon, I rounded the corner toward the Merritt Parkway—there would be no further traffic lights after this. The road was littered with glistening leaves and the streetlights reflected off the glossy surface. Out of the corner of my eye, I saw something move. That's when it all went wrong. My life would never be the same after that.

I heard a dull thud and all at once the car spun out of control. What is happening? I wondered as I desperately attempted to steady the Sunbird and right its direction. When it finally came to a stop, my body was trembling in shock. I took a deep breath and looked up to see what might have caused me to swerve. I fully expected to see a deer, which was commonplace along that stretch of road. Instead, I spotted a body lying face down on the pavement. Blood was surging through my veins, the adrenaline pumping my heart. I bounded out of the car and flew to the body. His shirt had ridden up on his back and I could see that he was breathing. I kneeled down beside him and placed my hand on his back—he was cold. So, I removed my windbreaker and covered his bare skin with my jacket, trying to protect him from the rain. My head was reeling. I didn't know what to do. Looking up into the black sky, I felt the icy drops pelting my cheeks. Dear God, please help him, I prayed.

Before long, other cars stopped by to assess the situation. People gathered, asking what had happened. I could feel the fear as blood pulsed through my veins. My agitation grew.

"Someone please call an ambulance. He needs help, now!" I screamed.

That was when I spotted the priest. An immediate sense of relief washed over me as I approached him. He would understand; he would comfort me. My faith had always been a central focus of my life. I looked up to the priests in my life to give guidance and support. I sought their counsel and wisdom in all I did. But it was much more than that for me. I had already been accepted as a seminarian for the Diocese of Bridgeport, Connecticut. I had begun my formation to become a priest. This man would be a brother priest in the very near future. Surely, he would be able to help. That thought calmed my frayed nerves. I didn't recognize him, but I knew that I had found a brother to help me get through the chaos of the moment. With tears in my eyes, I reached my hand out to him.

"Father, I don't know what happened…"

"Don't tell me. Tell the police," he snapped at me. His clipped voice sliced through my heart. Then he turned and walked away.

I stood there dumbfounded, not understanding what just happened. How could he just walk away from me? I need his help—I need to talk to him.

In a daze, I walked back to the boy lying on the ground. I kneeled beside him once again. Why is it taking so long for help to arrive? The police car pulled up before the ambulance. The officer pulled me away from the boy and peppered me with questions. He wasn't rude or angry—he simply took information down on his pad. While we were talking, the ambulance arrived and there was a flurry of activity around the boy. I froze as I watched the scene unfold, no longer answering questions. The officer put his hand on my shoulder.

"Why don't we get you out of the rain? I think I've gotten enough information for now," he said as he led me to the police car. "Take a seat and catch your breath."

When the car door slammed shut, my entire body shook. Hard as I tried, I could not gain control. There were no tears, not until later. I wrapped both arms around myself, and although the heater was on full blast, I could not get warm. I stared out the window in disbelief. Paramedics surrounded the boy—he was laid onto the stretcher and wheeled into the van. The flashing red and yellow lights reflected on the wet pavement, the police car, and the ambulance. They were all around me. Soon, the ambulance drove off, sirens blaring. Everything seemed to be moving in slow motion. The policemen interviewed those gathered, and then he walked over to my Sunbird and inspected it.

When the officers got into the squad car, I could think of nothing but the boy.

"Is...is he going to be all right? How bad is it?" I asked.

"He's in good hands now, son. I'm sure they are doing all they can to help him."

After a few more questions, the officer seemed satisfied. "Your car looks fine. Are you all right to drive home?"

"Yeah, I'm OK. What happens now?" I asked.

"It's clear that you weren't drinking or speeding, so you are free to go on your way. Come to the station tomorrow morning and you can sign the accident report. Are you sure, you can drive?"

"I'm sure. Thank you, Officer."

Thankfully, the few people who gathered had dissipated. I walked over to my car, which had spun around and was facing the opposite direction. I couldn't even tell it had been in an accident until I got to the door. There, on the driver's side quarter panel, was a softball-sized indentation just behind the headlight. My breath caught in my throat—I stood still as a statue. I heard the policeman call out to me and I turned to tell him I was fine.

Behind the wheel once again, I started my car and drove toward home. I recall going through the motions, not truly processing what had just happened. My mind was blank as I drove into my parents' driveway ten minutes later. I turned the key and the Sunbird was quiet. Resting my hands on the wheel, I realized I didn't remember the drive home. When I finally got out of the car, I didn't dare look at the dent in the Sunbird.

Feeling like a zombie, I found my way to the bedroom and undressed. Before long, I found myself curled under the bed covers with images of the accident swirling in my mind. Eyes wide open, I stared into the darkness.

Elusive Light

You keep track of all my sorrows.
You have collected all my tears in your bottle.
You have recorded each one in your book.

—Psalm 56:8

4
DOA

I don't remember falling asleep that night, but when morning came, I awoke to an overwhelming feeling of dread. As my mind slowly returned to consciousness, violent images from the night before flooded my mind. It wasn't a nightmare. It was real. It happened. It was as if a two-ton elephant was sitting on my chest. No matter how hard I tried, I could not fill my lungs. It felt as if I was suffocating. Garnering all the strength I could muster, I rose from the bed and padded out to the kitchen to pour myself a cup of coffee. Mom and Dad were already up and greeted me.

"Good morning, Mario," Mom sang. "How was your concert?"

"It was good, but very loud," I responded, trying to get more caffeine into my system. I tried to work up the courage to tell them what had happened. I didn't know what to say. My thoughts were jumbled as images of the night before flashed in my mind. Nearing the bottom of my mug, I lifted my head and spoke.

"Mom, Dad, I got into a car accident last night."

Both heads turned to face me, but no words were spoken.

"I was driving home from the concert when a guy crossed the road right in front of me. I hit him."

"Is he all right?" my mother asked.

"I…I don't know. They took him away in an ambulance. The police told me to come to the station this morning."

"Oh my God, Mario."

The three of us sat at the table not knowing what to say or do. I rose from my seat and placed my mug in the dishwasher.

"I'm going to take a shower. Then I'll head to the Fairfield Police Station. They need me to sign the accident report. Will you come with me?"

"Of course, we will," Mom replied as she wrapped her arms around me. Her unconditional love comforted me even though I felt unworthy. How could anyone love me after what I've done?

I hoped a hot shower would help lift the fog that clouded my mind. The warm spray on my neck and shoulders was a balm to my wounded heart, but it did little to release the tightness in my muscles. Every part of my body pulsed with tension. The water began to turn cold, so I stepped out of the tub and toweled myself dry. Going through the motions, I dressed and walked back to the kitchen. Dad already had his jacket on and keys in his hand.

The sun shined brightly after the rainy night before. If not for the heaviness in my chest, I would have enjoyed the crisp fall weather. The foliage unfolded its colors of gold, orange, and brilliant red as we passed through our neighborhood. Silently, we drove the very route I had taken the night before. Few people were on the road that early Saturday morning. We drove past the university and headed into town. The police station was a quaint building near the town center—a picturesque gazebo graced the square. Dad parked the car, then we climbed the steps to enter the station. I identified myself and, after a brief wait, we were escorted to a desk.

The officer was businesslike but not rude. He summarized the accident report and asked if I agreed with their assessment. I nodded and he handed me a pen to sign my name.

"OK, that's it," he said as he filed the report. "You're free to go."

"Thanks, but what about the boy?" I asked.

"What do you mean?"

"How is he? Is he going to be all right?"

"Oh, he was DOA. Sorry," the officer responded.

"DOA? I don't understand," I said, confusion painted on my face.

"Dead on arrival."

My head spun at hearing those words. It never occurred to me that he might die. I couldn't breathe. I sat there staring ahead blankly.

"Are you all right, kid? Can I get you some water?"

"What? Oh, no, I...I'm sorry."

"Look, I thought you knew," he said. "There have been no charges filed against you. You weren't speeding or drinking. It was just an unfortunate accident. Go home and get some rest."

We left the station and walked to the car. None of us said a word. We were all in shock. I barely remember the drive home. Dad pulled the car into the garage, and I mindlessly climbed the stairs, walked down the hall to my room, and closed the door. I sat on my bed and gazed at the crucifix hanging above the headboard. The weight of the news I just received came bearing down on me. A heaviness crushed my mind, my body, and my spirit. My eyes grew wet as hot tears flowed down my cheeks. My body shook and I sobbed, barely able to gasp for air. How could this have happened? How could he die? I don't understand.

I'm not sure how long I remained on my bed crying. When the intensity waned, I looked toward my bookshelf and spotted the bible I had since high school. It was geared toward teenagers—it had pictures and lessons throughout it, applying scriptures to modern-day events. I had stuffed it with mementos and photos. It contained so many memories of my teenage years. I reached for it and it fell open on my lap. I read the passage that stared back at me.

> Don't be afraid, for I have ransomed you;
> I have called you by name;
> You are mine.
> When you go through deep waters and great trouble,
> I will be with you.
> When you go through rivers of difficulty,
> You will not drown!
> When you walk through the fire of oppression,
> You will not be burned up,
> The flames will not consume you.
> For I am the Lord your God,
> And I love you.
> Do not be afraid, for I am with you.
> Isaiah 43:1-5

Time stood still. Gazing through my tears, I read words I had sung so many times before. The muscle memory in my fingers formed the chords on the neck of an imaginary guitar as I felt the frets. The melody and harmonies blended perfectly within my mind. I closed my eyes and lifted my head. I could actually hear the notes swirling around me. I had sung this song at countless Masses, retreats, and funerals. "Be not afraid. I go before you always. Come follow me and I will give you rest." My voice had been the source of comfort for worshipers at so many events. Now, these words were being sung to me from the pages opened before my eyes. Strong arms held me in their warm embrace and gently rocked me. I took a deep, cleansing breath and exhaled. At that moment, I could almost hear the words: It's going to be all right. You're going to be OK, Mario. I love you.

For the briefest of moments, I believed what I heard. But those reassuring words and the comfort they provided would soon dissipate. After composing myself as best I could, I opened the door to my bedroom and walked to the kitchen. My sisters stood at the top of the stairs and suddenly stopped speaking when they saw me approaching. I expected them to reach out or comfort me. But the look of pity on their faces said it all. I'm sure they didn't know what to say or do. In some ways, they were experiencing the trauma as well—everyone in my family was. But I couldn't grasp that. I was too fragile—something would have been better than nothing. I felt a cold grip on my heart as I imagined their judgment. I know now that was far from the truth, but I was broken. I took everything as a sign of my guilt. I desperately needed to be held, to be reassured that I was loved and lovable. Instead, my darkest thoughts were reinforced. I was the instrument of death.

Give sorrow words.
The grief that does not speak
Whispers the o're-fraught heart, and bids it break.

—William Shakespeare

5
MASS

    I isolated the rest of the weekend. I couldn't bear to face any of my friends after what I had done. The darkness was all-consuming, and I couldn't find my way out of the gloom. The sluggish passage of time was excruciating. I wallowed in a cocoon that blocked out the light. By Sunday evening, I desperately needed to get out of my own way. I decided to go to the 7:00 p.m. Mass on campus. I was a student leader of the folk group for years and the community of friends with whom I sang became one of my greatest supports. Familiar faces in the congregation made it feel like home and many of us would gather afterward for pizza and beer. If there was any place on campus where I felt safe, it was at the Loyola Chapel.

    I braced myself for trauma as I approached my Pontiac Sunbird for the first time since the accident. The car that was a symbol of my adulthood and freedom now carried images of death. Inserting the key in the lock, I glanced at the front quarter panel. The softball-sized dent stared back at me accusingly. I could barely see it in the late afternoon light of autumn. I took a deep breath and got behind the wheel once again. I was on autopilot—my body knew the way to campus without a thought. On a normal Sunday, I would have loaded my guitar case in the trunk and been the first to arrive at rehearsal before Mass. But not that day.

I planned to sneak into the chapel and sit in the back corner, obscured from anyone's vision. I hoped not to be noticed. The chapel was in the basement of a dorm, and there was always a flurry of activity in the halls that led to it. When I neared the Campus Ministry offices, Father Moy spotted me and guided me into his office.

"Mario," he exclaimed as he pulled me in, engulfing me in a hug. "Are you all right? Come sit down—talk to me."

I didn't realize he knew what had happened. Having been off campus and out of contact with my friends, I assumed that no one knew of my accident. But someone had contacted him, which meant that everyone knew. It felt like my world was closing in on me once again. A shadow engulfed me, darkening my vision, light obscured from my eyes. I sat on the couch beside the priest, but I didn't know what to say.

"You can stay here until Mass begins," Father Moy said. "This way you won't have to answer any questions."

Almost immediately, I felt relief from the pounding in my temples. Then a familiar face poked his head into the room. My best friend since high school came to the office to ask about me. I stood and Paul, not one for hugging, put his arm around me and embraced me tightly. Moments passed with no words spoken. Then Paul broke the silence.

"You OK, man? I'm so sorry."

"Yeah, I guess. I don't know what to feel, except bad."

"I can't even imagine how you feel," he said. "If you need

anything, I'm here. You know that, right?"

I nodded and sat back down on the couch. Paul and I had been friends throughout high school. We were inseparable. But at that time, he and I were in the midst of a cool place in our friendship. We both applied to become resident advisors. He was accepted; I was not. In my insecurities, I often felt that I fell short of his talent, leadership, and intelligence. These feelings were unconscious. On the surface, I was envious. Despite that, we truly loved one another. We'd always been there for each other, no matter our differences. His unconditional support at that moment meant everything to me. It gave me the strength to face the rest of my friends. So, when it came time for Mass, we entered the chapel together. I scanned the back pews for a place to hide. However, my plan to quietly slip in unnoticed was thwarted.

The folk group had always performed directly beside the altar in the sanctuary. That Sunday, they decided to experiment with the acoustics from the back of the chapel. They placed the guitars, microphones, and music stands in the last few pews and stood facing the front. When I saw them, I froze with fear. Sweat beaded on my forehead. My feet were lead blocks cemented to the floor. Silently, Paul placed his hand on my shoulder.

The director spotted me immediately. She rushed to give me a hug. Just a few feet away from the singers, she held me in her arms. Mrs. Benson was like a mother to all the singers, and resting in the comfort of her embrace was exactly what I needed.

"Why don't you sit with us during Mass, Mario?"

"No, that's OK. I can't sing tonight. I just need to be here."

"Of course. You don't have to sing. But you can sit with us, with your friends who love you very much. We've all been praying for you. Let us be here for you. Come, come sit with us."

Turning to the choir, I saw the faces of my friends draw me in, their eyes filled with compassion. Thankfully, no one said a word as I took a seat. Mrs. Benson went on with the rehearsal, practicing the songs for Mass. I was grateful I didn't have to explain anything or answer that awful question: How are you? Are you OK? I sat amidst my choir and let the melodies and harmonies weave into my heart and soul. With my eyes closed, I let the music begin the healing process I so desperately needed and got lost in the songs I loved so well. The familiarity of the Mass worked its magic. The ritual that I knew like my own hand soothed my aching heart. There were no surprises and I rested in a familiar spiritual home.

It was customary for the choir to sing a meditation song after Communion. As people processed up the aisle to receive the Eucharist, Mrs. Benson sidled up next to me and looked directly into my eyes.

"We're singing 'This Much I Love You,' Mario. We're dedicating it to you. Why don't you sing the solo verses like you usually do?"

"What? No…no, I can't do that. How can you ask me to sing tonight?"

"You don't have to sing if you don't feel strong enough. I know this song means a great deal to you. I thought it might help ease your pain. Greg is ready to sing the verses if you'd rather not. Just think about it. If you change your mind, just nod your head when it comes time. He'll drop out."

It was such a simple, yet outrageous offer. But Mrs. Benson was right; the song had always touched me deeply. I had sung it on retreats and was comforted by its pure childlike lyrics. The guitars played the introduction, and the choir began the refrain. Much to my surprise, the music swirled within my chest and filled my heart with light. I sat up on the back of the pew and sang along. Mrs. Benson and I locked eyes, then I nodded. A broad smile spread across her face, and she winked at me. In the back of the chapel, with the entire congregation facing the front, I was able to sing without being the center of attention. I closed my eyes and let the music flow from deep within me.

This much I love you.
This much I really care.
This much I love you.
And I'll always be right there.

The song ends with the soloist spreading his arms wide as Jesus did on the cross. After the refrain, I sang the final phrase a cappella: This much I love you, as he bowed his head and died.

There was not a sound in the chapel following my last note. My eyes were closed throughout the song as I let myself get lost in the presence of God. In the silence, I slowly opened my eyes. Each person in the choir had tears streaming down their cheeks. Looks of admiration and love engulfed me.

Looking back on it, the lyrics reek of sentimentality; it's a style of faith that causes me to roll my eyes. It turns me off. But in that moment, I felt at one with my God—in my suffering and in my need. Hearing the strum of the last chord on the guitars, I felt arms embracing me; engulfing me in their warmth. The choir surrounded me and cried with me that night. It was difficult to stand before people whom I loved, bearing the shame for what I had done. Their opinion of me mattered and I feared losing their love. For the first time since the accident, I didn't fear their judgment. Layer by layer, through the unconditional love shown to me, the self-loathing that plunged me into darkness was peeled away. They embraced me both figuratively and literally.

Can I see another's woe, and not be in sorrow too?
Can I see another's grief,
and not seek for kind relief?

—Sir William Blake

6
THE FUNERAL

The funeral Mass was held at St. Thomas Aquinas Church in Fairfield, Connecticut. It was a painful coincidence since my dear cousin Frank was pastor of the parish and would say the Mass. Making matters more difficult was that I was head of youth ministries at the church. The boy who died could have been one of the high school students in my charge. So many of them knew him; some went to school with him. And there I was, their leader, the one who caused his death. I couldn't bear facing these wonderful young people whom I had come to love. I felt as if I had betrayed them, let them down. I didn't have the skills or emotional maturity to sort out my myriad feelings. I was so ashamed. I believed that I was the instrument of death, and therefore, should suffer punishment of some kind.

At the same time, I was drawn to my spiritual home. St. Thomas was my parish church. I was actively involved in all parish ministries. I was friends with each of the priests and socialized with them on a regular basis. And of course, my cousin, Frank was my mentor. I had admired him and sought to emulate him as long as I could remember. I spent as much time at St. Thomas as I did on the university campus.

The fact that I was formally enrolled with the Diocese of Bridgeport as a candidate for priesthood complicated matters. I had begun spiritual direction with one of the priests at St. Thomas a year before. I had kept my intentions private. No one in my family knew of my plans except for Fr. Frank. I told none of my friends at the university, not even my buddies. I hoped to have as normal a college experience as possible. If my classmates knew I was in the seminary program, they would have treated me differently. My vocation, my calling was intensely precious to me. I needed to keep it private until I was ready to share it.

Each of these factors created layers of complexity in my grief. Each placed weight upon my already burdened shoulders. By itself, the tragedy of that night was profound. Adding the many circumstances of my life multiplied my shame and guilt. At night, I curled up in the fetal position and buried my head under the bed covers. I wanted nothing more than to hide from the world, but especially from all those whom I loved. I couldn't face my siblings, my parents, my classmates, or the students in my youth group.

Alongside my need to isolate was the desire, the need to be with my community. I desperately needed to be with my university buddies. I sought a space where I was unconditionally loved, embraced, and held in their hearts. I also felt the chasm between my deep bond with St. Thomas Church. When I heard the funeral would take place there, I was devastated once again. The confluence of my traumatic accident and my spiritual home was overwhelming. How could his funeral be there, at my church? It was my safe space, and from then on it would always be associated with my most painful experience. The injustice of the circumstances was a crushing weight on my heart.

In my confusion, I resolved to attend the funeral. I wanted to mourn with the family, with my students, and with my parish. As painful as it would be, I knew in my heart that I should be there to usher him into eternal life. My faith comforted me somewhat in that we would celebrate a Mass of Resurrection for a life cut short—unnaturally short. When I shared my intentions with my cousin, Fr. Frank, he looked at me with a pained expression. His eyes were soft and heavy-lidded, and his smile was almost imperceptible.

"Oh, Mario. I can only imagine the anguish you are feeling. Your desire to be there despite how painful it would be, reveals your compassionate heart. But you cannot attend the funeral. The family is mourning the tragic loss of their son and brother. Although I know they do not blame you for what happened, it is a wound that is freshly cut. The Mass must be focused on them and their love for Vance. Your presence would detract from that. Can you understand this?"

My mouth agape, I stared blankly at him. Eyes welling with tears, I looked away in shame. My face flushed red as I felt the heat of the blood pulsing in my temples. I am such a monster. Even Fr. Frank believes I shouldn't be at the funeral.

He reached out and pulled me into his embrace. He stroked my hair as I sobbed against his shoulder.

"You'll be OK, Mario. I promise you. Just let it out. I'm always here for you."

But I did not believe him. I was lost and I didn't know how to find my way back home.

Life seems sometimes like nothing more than a series
of losses, from beginning to end. That's the given.
How you respond to those losses,
what you make of what's left,
that's the part you have to make up as you go.

—Katharine Weber

7
UNRAVELING

The weeks and months following the car accident found me wandering as if in a fog. There was no clarity of vision or emotion beyond the abyss of torturous pain. I attended classes but absorbed nothing. I followed my routine, went through the motions of an ordinary college senior. Friends met at the Stag-her Inn, the campus pub, to drink or listen to music. As vice-president of the Glee Club, I attended the officers' meetings discussing the minutia of club politics. Each of us in attendance spoke passionately about the goings on. They argued over the proper action to be taken or direction for performances, repertoire, or the spring travel season. I sat listening to each argument at a distance. The voices echoed in my mind.

Shortly after that evening, I quit the Glee Club. Singing was everything to me. I was obsessed with performing. My best friend, Paul could not understand. Why would I quit something that had always brought me such joy? I couldn't explain it. What I knew was that the inane arguments meant nothing to me. Suddenly, I had little patience for pettiness. I found myself letting go of many clubs and activities. I shed anything that felt like an obligation. I distanced myself from acquaintances who seemed foolish or shallow. There was no room for small talk. If we didn't meet on a deeper level, we didn't meet at all.

The ever-happy Mario went underground. Bitterness and cynicism surfaced and colored my worldview. As the holidays neared, the university campus was aglow with twinkling lights and Christmas music. Finals were quickly approaching, and my homework piled up. But I remained cloaked in darkness. None of it mattered to me. How did a failing grade compare to the death of a high school kid? Nearing the end of the semester, I exited the science building and ran into my psychology professor. Fr. McGrath was revered on campus. A wisdom figure, one could not accuse him of being warm or cuddly. However, he was passionate about his discipline and his lectures were awe-inspiring. Fr. McGrath addressed me directly.

"Mario."

"Hello, Father."

"How are you, Mario?"

"I…I'm OK, I guess."

Fire in his eyes, he gripped my shoulders, his face inches from mine.

"No, Mario. How are you, really?"

My defenses melted away. For the briefest of moments, light dispelled the darkness.

"To be honest, I don't know. Everyone expects me to be over it, to be back to normal. It's like everyone has moved on. But I'm still stuck where I was."

He raised his voice and spoke with gravitas.

"No! You shouldn't be over it. You need to feel it. No one has the right to tell you to get over it. You are the only one that matters at this moment. Do you understand?"

Despite his intensity, I felt relief wash over me. He let me off the hook.

"Yes, Father. I think so. Thank you."

"Listen, finals are coming up. What are you going to do?"

"I have no idea. I can't concentrate in any of my classes. I feel completely lost."

"OK. Then don't take them."

"I don't understand. I need to take my finals. I have to graduate."

"But you don't have to take them now. You can postpone them. Take them in January or later. I will take care of it. Your job right now is to take care of Mario. Do you understand?"

"Yes, Father. Thank you, I…"

He pulled me into a rough hug, and then walked into the science building. I stood there, dazed, but relieved. For the first time in many weeks, someone truly saw me. McGrath didn't allow me to give a rote answer to how I was feeling. He knew better and made sure I knew. He gave me permission to grieve. He made a space for me to hurt and to acknowledge my anguish. For the first time, I felt it was all right to feel the pain. I didn't have to pretend. While the rest of the world moved on, I had only begun to experience the depth of my trauma. No one had the right to expect more from me. I was the priority.

I took a deep breath of the cold December air as I glanced at the barren trees, their brittle branches fanned into the winter sky. The chill was somehow comforting, and my heart ached a bit less. But that moment of relief did not last much longer. College-age students hold no space for sadness, let alone grief. I continued to go through the motions, singing in the Christmas concert, at midnight Mass, and attending the end-of-semester gatherings. Before I knew it, the next semester had begun. The hints of spring brought renewed hope and glimpses of normalcy. I was a second-semester senior. My graduation was only months away.

My bubbly personality peaked through the gloom more often and I began to look toward the future. Given my interest in becoming a priest, my schedule included several advanced theology courses. I enjoyed debating philosophical points and defending opposing theories. One day in March, I sat at my desk in my favorite professor's class. Several of my dearest friends contributed to a spirited and dynamic discussion. The topic was God's benevolence—his grace given freely to the world.

"Grace is that which sustains us in times of trouble," Tim said.

"It's what transforms the human condition from original sin to goodness and opens us up to a healthy relationship with God," Joan added.

"Right," Tim continued. "Grace is the vehicle through which we as humans touch the face of God, and he in turn, embraces us along our journey through life."

These were beautiful statements borne out of faith and based on the readings for class. Less than a year before, I would have chimed in and carried the discussion further, claiming that God's never-ending grace heals our wounds, brings light to the darkness of our lives, and gives meaning to that which we cannot comprehend. It was truly what I believed. But as they spoke, I felt a physical revulsion to the concept of grace—to God's all-embracing love. Where is that grace in my life? Where is God throughout my dark night of the soul? When did he come to comfort me in my agony?

"This is all bullshit!" I exclaimed.

All eyes turned to me. There was an audible intake of

air. I could feel the shock reverberate throughout the room. But I could not stop the flood of resentment flowing from my lips.

"Can you seriously say that God's grace takes away human suffering—that grace washes original sin away? Given all the pain and suffering in our world, in our very lives, how can you be so deluded? God doesn't care about us humans. That is if there even is a God. He wound the clock and set the world in motion, then sits back and lets us suffer. If that's grace, then we had better find a more suitable solution to human suffering."

Each phrase expressed the depth of my pain and my struggle with a faith that was deeply rooted. I was furious with God, and it was pouring forth like venom. No one in that classroom could escape its sting. A vacuous silence followed my diatribe. Then, moments later the room erupted in counter arguments. Tim's hand gripped my shoulder from behind. Joan's eyes bore into me with compassion. She could feel my pain. The professor stood and without skipping a beat, jumped in with a twinkle of sympathy in his eyes.

"Mario has a point. What of free will? If God interfered with the workings of the world, wouldn't that block free will? How do we reconcile the suffering of the world with God's benevolence? How, indeed, does God interact with the world? These questions have been the basis of theological arguments throughout the ages. Flowery discussions about grace are all well and good in theory. But the human condition is fraught with pain and suffering. We can spend our entire lives seeking the comfort of God's grace."

Dr. Thiel disarmed me by acknowledging my raging emotions within the framework of our theological discussion. He didn't embarrass me by calling attention to my emotional outburst. The professor took the kernel of philosophy acknowledging its validity while letting me know it was OK to question God's grace, His love, His very presence in my life.

The realization of my emotional argument crept into my consciousness almost immediately. I was embarrassed and wanted nothing more than to crawl under my desk. What is wrong with me? How can I treat my friends like this? I was so disrespectful to Dr. Thiel. The remainder of the class passed at a snail's pace. I had checked out, sitting there in my world of darkness. I couldn't see or hear clearly. Everyone seemed miles away, their voices barely registering in my consciousness. When the bell rang, I was startled out of my distant hiding place. My friends gathered around me. I felt their touch and heard the sweet timber of sympathetic voices. I was mortified. I needed to get away from everyone, to find a quiet place and cry, if the tears would even come.

There were numerous occasions when my emotional outbursts were in no way proportional to the situation at hand. Although I sought counseling at the student center, my inner turmoil spilled over my protective mask of control. I could physically feel myself unraveling, and I feared I would never return to normalcy.

SACRED & PROFANE

I sat facing the psychologist for the fourth or fifth time wondering if any of this was worth it. What is there to say that I haven't already said? I described the accident in vivid detail. Every torturous moment was emblazoned in my memory. I had shared my deep sadness and sense of isolation. We spoke of my faith in God and His place in the Calvary I endured on a daily basis. What more was there to uncover?

After an interminable period of silence, he asked, "What

happened? Why are you shut down?"

I recounted the episode from theology class earlier that day. As I spoke, my voice became louder and my gestures more expressive. Wound up like a jack in the box, I could feel myself getting tighter and tighter. I knew I was close to exploding so I cut myself off mid-sentence, my fists in tight balls. I shook with emotion.

"What? What are you feeling, Mario?"
"Nothing. I just feel so…" My words trailed off.
"So what? What do you feel?"
"I just…I am so…it's so fffff…"
"Say it. Don't hold back. So what?"
"FFFFFF…"
"Say it."
"Fuck," I whispered.
"What did you say?"
"FUCK, FUCK, FUCK!"
"That's it. Let it out."

My body shook more violently than before. But it was due to the tremendous release of tension. The dragon had been revealed and flames of anger spewed forth. Now that it had surface with no constraints, I couldn't stop the tirade. I was angry at my friends for treating me with kid gloves. I was angry that my senior year of college had been destroyed. I was angry that my grades had tanked. I was angry that activities I had always loved meant little or nothing to me. I was angry with God.

•••

Admitting my anger with God startled me. How could I, the good little boy, the young seminarian, be angry with God? That is simply not allowed. To understand how out of character my outburst was, I must tell you that up to that point in my life, I had never uttered a curse word. Hearing myself speak such a violently ugly profanity shocked me. The anguish and anger it revealed was powerful. My anger was the one true emotion that bound the rest of them within the prison of my psyche. But it was clear to me that anger with God had to be dealt with whether it was allowed or not. It was real. It was a valid emotion. Once named, I could not ignore it.

My simple faith had become complicated. Bible verses inspirational readings, or quotes lost their power. They did not comfort me in my darkness. Scripture no longer addressed the questions now in the forefront of my mind. The existence of evil and suffering in the world was at my door or in my heart. These were not abstract concepts. Suffering was personal, not something for faceless strangers in a faraway place. Suffering was within me.

The suffering of Christ never seemed so real. But at least there was meaning to His death. The salvation of the world depended upon it. What, then, was the meaning of my suffering? Why was I the instrument of death for this sixteen-year-old boy? What lesson was I to learn from this trauma?

What I didn't realize at the time, was that my safe, secure world had been shattered. My belief that everything would always work out for the best had been proven wrong. My perspective of the world changed the instant I received the news that Vance was DOA. A very different Mario had begun to emerge, and I didn't yet know who he was or what he believed. It was a profound loss of innocence.

How does one grieve a loss such as this? There is no individual to remember or miss. The concept of innocence is nebulous. It was a loss of comfort, of safety. How does one move forward when they don't feel safe or secure?

Elusive Light 67

On this bald hill the new year hones its edge.
Faceless and pale as china
The round sky goes on minding its business.
Your absence is inconspicuous,
Nobody can tell what I lack.

—Sylvia Plath, Parliament Hill Fields

8
A LIGHT DIMMED

As I have mentioned, Father Frank was not simply a beloved member of my family—he was my mentor and friend. Just a few months earlier, he experienced the unimaginable loss of both his parents and grandfather. I grieved with him, but certainly not in the same way. Nothing could compare with the tragic and senseless accident that led to the death of three family members. His sorrow ran deep. Even so, he did his best to guide me through my trauma. Most importantly, he showed me that I was loved and valued. He showed me that he loved me unconditionally.

More than a year later, Frank was still living his loss. He returned to his daily routine. His homilies continued to be inspired—he knew how to capture his congregants with stories they could relate to. He made us laugh with silly jokes or tales of family drama. But when Mass was over, he drew inward. The darkness settled in once again.

At that time, I had been accepted as a seminarian for the

Diocese Bridgeport in Connecticut. As a seminarian studying for the Catholic priesthood, I received weekly spiritual direction and gathered with other young men following the same path. While finishing up my undergraduate degree at Fairfield University, I was required to minor in philosophy and take a number of courses in religious studies. When I received news that I was appointed to the North American College in Vatican City, I was elated. The Vatican is the center of the Catholic Church. It was a great honor to be sent to Rome to study for the priesthood. Having never been in the seminary, there was so much about Church politics I did not understand.

Nonetheless, Fr. Frank ushered me into the seminary and sent me off to Vatican City to become a priest. I wanted nothing more than to follow in his footsteps—to be the beloved parish priest who was present at the most significant moments in people's lives: birth, marriage, and death. Frank gifted me with a four-volume set of breviaries—the books of prayer that all ordained people use each day from morning to evening. It was such an intimate gift that signified my membership in his holy brotherhood. His simple gesture told me that he believed in me, that we would someday be brother priests, serving side by side.

We wrote to each other often during my year in Rome. It was a challenging experience for me. Less than a year after my car accident, I found myself thousands of miles away from everyone I loved. My support network was suddenly gone. Phone calls were exorbitantly expensive, and mail took weeks to arrive. I suffered from homesickness and naïveté. I wasn't ready for the world of Church politics and the formal environment of Rome. Immersing myself into the Italian way of life was comfortable. However, the clerical world was an entirely foreign culture to which I could not adapt. Although I waited impatiently for his letters, and our phone calls were infrequent, they sustained me in my need. I sought his counsel many times over during that formative year. Frank was my rock.

When I left Rome the following June, I visited him immediately. My spirit had been broken by my experiences at the North American College in Vatican City. I believed that I had lost my faith and that the bishop did not care about my spiritual well-being. Living under constant scrutiny, I began to doubt my myself and my chosen path. The question of whether we were worthy of the priesthood loomed like a dark cloud over our heads. Had God truly chosen me to be his representative on earth? Was I worthy to be ontologically changed through ordination? The entire experience in Rome tapped into my already weakened self-image. Self-loathing regarding my sexuality resurfaced. It became intertwined with feelings of unworthiness. I believed I was undeserving of priesthood and that being gay was shameful.

I poured out my heart, describing in great detail, each conflict, doubt and struggle. In response, Frank was gentle and kind. He never told me to buck up, put my head down and forge ahead. He listened and walked with me, sharing in my pain. It was true compassion—from the Latin, compassionem, to suffer with, and that is what he did.

Immersed in my own internal turmoil, it took me weeks before I suspected something was not right with Frank. While in Assisi, I used the little money I had to commission a hand-woven stole for Frank. A stole is part of the ceremonial vestment a priest wears to say Mass or administer a sacrament. Frank had done so much for me. I wanted to get him something unique, a gift that demonstrated how special he was to me. I was so excited to give it to him. When I presented it to him, I waited in eager anticipation as he unwrapped the gift. His reaction to the gift was not what I expected. He lifted the woven stole from the box and held it in his hands. He fingered the weave, ran his hand over the ruby red Jerusalem cross that embellished each side. He looked up at me with watery eyes, a wan smile on his face. I could tell Frank was moved by my gift, but there was no excitement. It was almost as if he knew he'd never get to wear it.

It was then that I saw it. There was a darkness in Frank's eyes. The ever-present twinkle was missing, as if the spark had gone out. Something was very wrong. It was more than the heaviness of grief that had become his constant companion during that last year. For the first time, I noticed he was physically frail. His normal robust stature had abandoned him. I admonished myself. How could I have not seen this? How selfish of me to pour all my troubles onto him?

As the weeks passed, he was often exhausted, tiring from ordinary tasks. I visited with him every day, helping him with little things. I set up for Mass, retrieved his breviaries, and fetched pen and paper for homilies. Frank's needs outweighed my seemingly trivial struggles in Rome. I became his right hand. One day, he was weaker still. His mind wasn't as sharp as usual, and his balance was off. I didn't know what to do, so I stayed close by, at the ready should he fall.

"Mario, something is not right," he said gasping for air. His breathing was labored. "I think we should go to the hospital. Can you call my doctor? The number is written on the pad near the phone."

His doctor told me to drive him to the emergency room at St. Vincent's Hospital. He would meet us there so we wouldn't need to check in. Frank asked me to help him get to the restroom to fix his hair and clean up a bit. Standing at the sink, comb in hand, he lost his balance, so I propped him up. He passed gas and was embarrassed. I could tell he was mortified when he apologized.

"Don't worry about that, Frank. How many times has

your father done that with pride and laughed about it? It's a family tradition."

He let out a forced chuckle. I tried to make him laugh to ease his shame. It was all about the loss of dignity. He wasn't ready to let go of that. I didn't want to be there for it either. Frank was my hero. I wanted him to remain on a pedestal as the man I could one day become. His declining health took that away from both of us.

Once at the hospital, Frank's illness progressed rapidly. Diagnosed with non-Hodgkin's lymphoma, he had been in remission for years. But the disease had returned with a vengeance. I believe that his immeasurable grief opened the door for its resurgence and weakened his immune system. His decline progressed quickly. Each day brought more complications and the strain on his organs took a toll on him. It was unimaginable but within weeks, Frank was dead. To be honest, I don't remember when I got the news. My memory of his final days seems blocked. My journal entries from those weeks are filled with torturous visits and questioning God's will. Visiting Frank in his final days was almost too painful to bear.

I watched his steady and rapid decline. I barely had time to process the fact that he was dying before my eyes. The selfish part of me could not accept that my cousin, friend, and mentor was no longer there to guide me, to love me, to challenge me. There would never be anyone who could hold the same place in my life. We shared the same blood. He understood our family traditions and history. We shared a vocational journey that no one else in our family could understand. Frank and I were friends.

WALLS CLOSING IN

The funeral Mass was held at St. Thomas Aquinas Church. Once again, my family gathered there to mourn a beloved family member. Because Frank was a revered pastor, hundreds of parishioners were in attendance. The pews were packed with mourners, and people lined the side aisles and spilled into the vestibule. I was asked to do the first reading. When the time came, I composed myself and walked to the lectern. I stood silently for a moment and looked out at the sea of grieving faces. I could feel the swell of emotion brimming to the surface. No, don't lose your composure, Mario. Get it together, my inner voice shouted. I looked down at the very same Scripture verses I read for Frank's parents, my aunt, and two uncles. I took a deep breath and began to read with a powerful voice:

"The Souls of the just are in the hand of God, and no torment shall touch him."

I was on automatic pilot. I knew the reading by heart, and I read as if I were on stage, playing a part in a play. I couldn't entertain any of my emotions. If I had, all my composure would be lost. Before I knew it, I heard myself say, "The word of the Lord." I looked up from the lectionary and stepped down. I crossed in front of the altar, bowed, and returned to my pew without looking at the coffin. I couldn't bear it.

After Mass, the funeral procession led us to the chapel at the cemetery. My family gathered around the coffin at the mausoleum. The sweet perfume of lilies wafted through the air. Sprays of flowers dwarfed those of us gathered. Arrangements of roses, chrysanthemums, and gladiolas spilled over into every corner of the chapel. There was hardly enough room for all of us. We were numb as we watched row upon row of priests shuffling in. My emotions only seemed to intensify at this final ritual. Frank's siblings, our aunts, and uncles wailed as the final prayers were said. The crowd of mourners pressed in on them from every side. The prayers droned on with few people paying attention. Holy water was sprinkled on the coffin. Then the Bishop addressed the family and friends in attendance.

"Dearly beloved, how can we make sense of such a loss? Monsignor Frank Dell'Olio lived his life in the footsteps of Christ. His life was snuffed out much too soon. We mourn his passing but look to the future as we celebrate his life. He spent his priesthood serving God's people with an unrelenting passion, so I ask you to pray with me." He paused. "Let us pray that from Monsignor Dell'Olio's family, a call might be answered to fill his shoes and serve as a priest."

At that moment, I felt every eye focused on me. The crowd physically turned to look at me. Of course, I was that person. I was already studying to be a priest in Rome, no less. Fear gripped me as I felt my own will being ripped away. The ground beneath me began to crumble, just like my fragile decision to leave the seminary. All I could see were scores of eyes focused on me. Their expressions ranged from pity, to encouragement and admiration. It was way too much pressure. I could physically feel the weight of their gaze upon me. They would never understand my decision to leave. How could I disappoint them? I wondered if it was God's will. Perhaps it was a sign. My mother looped her arm into mine and sobbed into my chest.

"Fr. Frank was always so proud of you, Mario," she said quietly. "Thank God you are here to carry on for him." A steel cage slammed shut around my heart. It barred me from making any other choice.

REPRESSION

A few weeks later, I followed the routine of a second-year seminarian as if nothing had happened. My grief over the loss of my mentor was pushed deep into my subconscious. The trauma of the previous few years mingled with the fresh wound that Frank's death opened up.

The ritual of the Mass had always comforted me in times of need. In a similar way, following the routine of a seminarian filled that void. There was no need to think about my pain. I attended classes, read hundreds of pages for homework, and attended Mass. My spiritual director knew of my recent loss and offered an ear as well as sage advice. For the first few months, I was able to function normally. But my emotions couldn't remain buried for long.

My anger with God surfaced again. Alongside it was the familiar self-loathing. I believed I was unworthy to be a priest like Frank. Guilt over my car accident seeped through the cracks in my composure. Conflict with the Church's teaching on homosexuality confronted me at every turn. So many of my fellow seminarians had repressed their sexuality only to find it bursting through in the pressure cooker of the seminary walls.

A deep depression took hold. I was numb to all the pain as well as suffering the intensity of numerous losses in recent years. By the end of the semester, I couldn't go through the motions any longer. I had to get out of the seminary. I left the dream of priesthood behind. However, I continued to search for God in the vacuum it left.

What followed was years of redefining myself. Always certain that I would become a priest, I was confronted with the reality that I had no direction. I was a boat without a rudder, bobbing and weaving in the tumultuous surf. My inner turmoil continued to eat away at me.

It wasn't until I started teaching high school that I learned to love myself again. I had a purpose and a calling. I discovered that I was good at something other than ministry. My students were drawn to me and I dedicated myself to teaching and guiding them. I had something to offer the world.

Grief can be the garden of compassion.
If you keep your heart open through everything,
your pain can become your greatest ally
in your life's search for
love and wisdom.

—Rumi

9
FEAR OF LOSS

There's something called forbidden grief. The term is used to describe feelings of loss that are not recognized or validated by one's community or society at large. The individual experiencing that loss is left to face it alone since no one else knows of the loss or acknowledges it as grief. Forbidden grief can also be unrecognizable by the one experiencing it. A general feeling of heaviness or sadness can weigh on one's heart. The danger of forbidden grief is that it can often be repressed or denied. It can be associated with feelings of guilt that come from the lack of validation from one's community or family members. Why do I feel so sad? I have no right to feel this way? If only I were different, I would be happy.

Wrapped in guilt, my forbidden or closeted grief took root deep within my psyche. I believed that I was unworthy of happiness because of my identity. Everyone in my family, as well as my friends, were seemingly normal happy people. I had difficulty comparing myself with those I loved the most.

I grew up as a first-generation Italian boy. I am the youngest of four children born five years after my older brother and sister and seven years after my oldest sister. My siblings were only two years apart reaching each childhood milestone at similar times. By the time I came along, my experience of family life was more akin to being an only child. My siblings helped raise me and I looked to their lives as I dreamed about my future. They had boyfriends or girlfriends, went out on dates, and chose career paths. I lived vicariously through them. However, from an early age, I knew I was different. I didn't understand how or why that was so, but I felt it deep within me.

I recall sifting through black and white photographs of my parents' youth back in Italy. Beautiful young women and handsome men strolled in the piazza donning dresses and suits. The southern Italian coast shimmered in photographs with adolescent boys and girls playing at the shore. Wearing overly conservative swimsuits, they looked strangely funny to me. Even so, I was fascinated by the images of people from a world an ocean away. I found myself drawn to each of the young men in the pictures rather than the women. Their jocular smiles and muscular physiques fascinated me. I didn't understand why, but somehow, I knew it was wrong—something to be ashamed of. Although I was much too young to comprehend, it was the first clue to my divergent sexuality.

Throughout my high school years, I dated steadily. I always had a girlfriend, and I enjoyed each playful relationship. I went to no fewer than five proms. However, I was continually more concerned with the dating lives of my male friends. Looking back, I can see that I was eager to emulate them and copy their behavior with their dates. I became jealous of the time their girlfriends took away from me. I didn't realize it then, but I was covetous of our time alone, without their girlfriends. There was nothing sexual about my feelings, however, my emotional attachment was more than what was common for an ordinary friendship.

It wasn't until my university years that I realized that I might be gay. I didn't take to this revelation well. It was against all that I was taught as a child. A person grows up, gets married, and has children. The only alternative was to become a priest, and I believed in my heart that I was called to the priesthood. The concept of being gay was inconsistent with that calling as well as the image of a normal family. The battle within my heart and soul commenced and the fallout damaged my self-image. As it became clear that I was not like the rest of my family or friends, I felt isolated and lonely. I was faced with losing all whom I loved because of my sexuality. I believed they would no longer love me if they truly knew me. I could not risk losing them, so I remained silent. I couldn't take the chance of coming out.

Coming of age during the 1980s as a gay man was fraught with danger. The AIDS crisis decimated the gay communities throughout the country. Fear gripped healthcare workers. Politicians and church leaders preached against the evils of homosexuality. AIDS was God's retribution against such a depraved lifestyle. In the early years of the epidemic, little was known about how AIDS was contracted and spread. Gay men were vilified. Politicians campaigned to place gay men into camps to remove them from society. Coming out as gay was layered with prejudice and suspicion. Christian churches taught that homosexual behavior was sinful and condemned those who were not celibate.

In the face of these teachings, I had returned to priestly formation for the Jesuits. I still believed it was my calling. In the Catholic world, the Pope can issue documents or teachings to advise the faithful on matters of ethics or morality. Unless the

Pope states that a given teaching is infallible, and most are not, it is meant to help direct Catholics to live in communion with God. In October 1986, the Vatican issued a teaching concerning the pastoral care of homosexuals.

Before this document, the official teaching of the church separated homosexual acts from homosexual persons. The acts were evil. As long as an individual refrained from those acts, he was free from sin. The Halloween letter, as it was commonly known, changed the previous teaching in a significant way. It stated that the inclination of the homosexual person was oriented toward intrinsic moral evil, that it was in their nature to commit evil acts. It also stated that people shouldn't be surprised when acts of violence are committed against them when they fight for rights they should not have.

It was like a dagger to my heart. In one swipe of the pen, the Catholic Church took away my dream of priesthood as well as declaring that I was oriented toward moral evil. I was devastated. I could no longer, in good conscience, continue my formation toward priesthood. In my heart, I believed my church had turned its back on me. I had lost two foundational aspects of my life.

I spent years grieving the loss of a normal life, the loss of my dream of priesthood, and the loss of my image as a straight man. Identifying as gay put me at odds with the Church and all those I loved.

Beyond the negative confines of church teaching, I learned to accept my sexuality as a gift. I came to understand that love is the greatest gift in life, no matter what form it takes. I slowly gave myself permission to love, to let my heart feel attraction. Over time, I regained my positive attitude. I began to live again. But my concept of God necessarily evolved. Without conscious examination, the idea of the divine expanded. My

Catholic/Christian belief system didn't go away, but my spiritual journey was not limited to the scriptures or doctrine. If I believed the Catholic teaching regarding homosexuality, I could never attain a psychologically healthy self-image. To accept that I was intrinsically oriented toward moral evil would be to admit that I was disordered. That is the very language used in the Vatican document.

I knew I was a good and loving person and somehow needed to develop my sense of well-being. The Church forced me to move beyond its limited teaching on sexuality to find my self-worth. I never felt as if I was betraying my faith or God. It was more like getting to know someone over twenty or thirty years of marriage. My faith and I grew together into something uniquely beautiful and free. That evolution is what opened the space in my life for love. Letting go of the Church's destructive definition of who I was as a gay man allowed love to enter my life in a healthy and fruitful way.

Following a similar path toward priesthood, I met the person who would become my partner in life. With similar values and steadfast faith, our foundation was secure right from the start. Jim and I bonded over the wounds caused by our Church. We bore the scars of the teaching that labeled us as oriented toward moral evil. We experienced a great loss as we felt abandoned by an institution to which we hoped to dedicate our lives. The Church had held a central place throughout our lives. It was a significant loss for both of us. Together, we moved beyond the Church teaching and discovered mutual care and respect for one another as we journeyed through life together.

Every one of us is losing something precious to us. Lost opportunities, lost possibilities, feelings we can never get back again. That's part of what it means to be alive.
—Haruki Murakami

10
TRAUMA

What is traumatic or complicated grief? I never knew there was a term for this type of grief, but there it is. Traumatic grief often happens after a natural disaster or accident. The event usually has a great impact on one's life. It can fully disrupt the normal rhythm of life. It doesn't necessarily involve the loss of life, but the experience leaves the victim in a vulnerable place. The grief may be due to the loss of security or safety—the belief that one is secure and free from danger. Personal safety is a foundational element in how we interact with the world around us. When our security is on unsteady ground, we feel unbalanced. Feelings of anxiety, sadness, or anger can color all we encounter.

A pivotal event in my life did not involve the loss of life. Rather, it was the loss of a dream as well as a terrifying and traumatic event. Perhaps it was a mid-life crisis—a search for meaning or an escape from the responsibilities of life. In any case, before my sail across the ocean, I had regained my belief that circumstances in life would work themselves out for the best. Just as I did before my car accident. I didn't fear for my safety and my sense of adventure drove me to many exciting experiences. I was certain that the outcome would be filled with joyful exploits. The grief I experienced afterward was not only a loss of a dream, but a loss of innocence, once again. At forty years of age, I faced the possibility of death because of my adventurous spirit. By this time, I had been married to my husband for over ten years. Together, we embarked on what should have been an exciting journey across the ocean. I could never have anticipated the trauma that ensued.

The waves were crashing all around me, pushing me further away from the boat. The relentless onslaught of white water obscured my vision, assaulting me from every direction. I frantically kicked my legs to stay above the surface of the bottomless ocean. The shoreline was miles away, and I trembled in fear. I struggled to catch my breath as wave after wave struck my face. The taste of the salty sea scorched my already dehydrated mouth. I reached in vain for the white plastic garbage bag that was being tossed around in the surf. It contained all the important documents that I had salvaged—I had to get hold of it.

It was difficult to distinguish the white plastic from the frothy foam of the crashing waves. The bag was almost within my grasp when I was suddenly pulled under. I was disoriented, submerged beneath the tumbling waters.

The din of the violent waves was thunderous. Terrified, I fought against the force of the surf that pushed and twisted my already weakened body. Resisting the impulse to panic, I battled my way back to the top. I needed air. Gathering my remaining strength, I propelled myself through the tumultuous waters. I pierced the surface and gasped as oxygen inflated my burning lungs.

I was in the middle of the turbulent waters of the coral reef without a life jacket, fighting to stay afloat. I had lost sight of the bag and was desperately scanning for it when it popped back up. This time I grabbed a hold of it. At least we had our passports and the little cash we had brought with us. But at that moment I felt no relief. Rather, an irrepressible anger welled up within me as I looked up at the gray sky and screamed, "What the hell have you done to us?"

I erupted in anger towards God. How could he have let this happen to us? My worst nightmare was coming true. We were miles from the shore, getting pummeled into the coral reefs. My body shook as I felt my childhood fear of the open ocean welling inside me. Is this how our lives end? Would we survive? Or will we end up drowning before help arrives?

None of it made sense to me. How did we end up here? What possessed us to leave San Francisco? We had successful jobs, a beautiful home, and a community of friends whom we loved. We traveled to exotic places, and each held its unique allure. We fantasized about what it would be like to live in Italy, Ireland or Spain. On a recent vacation, the beauty of the Caribbean had seduced us. The sun's rays sparkled on the clear blue water. Sailing from island to island and feeling the warm breeze caress our faces, there seemed to be no downside to living in that part of the world. After years of dreaming of retiring to an exotic destination, we took a leap of faith.

Our survival hung in the balance as we fought for our lives in the once beautiful waters that had drawn us to the Caribbean. Their beauty had beguiled us into leaving everything behind to live in a tropical paradise. How could it all have gone so wrong?

•••

Months before, my husband, Jim, and I chartered a sailboat, hopping from island to island in the Caribbean. It was an idyllic respite from the daily grind in San Francisco. I dreamed of leaving it all behind and starting a new life in a tropical paradise. I had been working seven days a week, while Jim's job required him to travel for weeks on end. I was done with the rat race, and I continually sought ways to jump ship. All I wanted to do was run away from it all, and I began a manic search for our dream life on the islands. Before long, we had bought a fifty-foot sailboat, quit our jobs, and set sail for St. Thomas, V.I.

However, the maiden journey did not turn out as we planned. Sailing from Norfolk, Virginia in mid-November proved to be a disaster. The plan was to sail to Bermuda, then head south to St. Thomas. We encountered one storm after another as we crossed the ocean, and we were plagued by mechanical issues—a fire in the helm, broken navigation equipment, and a malfunctioning rudder. Ultimately, we were unable to steer the boat. With a hurricane developing in the eastern Atlantic, our situation became increasingly dire. We had to make a decision. Storms raged, the seas rose higher, and the winds became increasingly stronger. We knew we were in danger and set off the EPIRB (Emergency Position-Indicating Radio Beacon,) an SOS signal to alert the Coast Guard.

Jim and I sheltered ourselves in a dry corner of the crew cabin, trying to get warm. We had not slept throughout the days at sea and were both physically and emotionally exhausted. We were anxiously awaiting the Coast Guard.

Time passed slowly. Our clothes were soaked, and our flesh was cold, so we clung to each other to preserve body heat. I turned to look at Jim at one point to see his eyes were wide open, glassy, and red; he was staring up at the ceiling. I don't know if he was praying, crying, or coming to terms with our hopeless situation. But it was clear that he was struggling, almost as if he was saying goodbye to life during these final moments. When he noticed me looking at him, he just said, "I love you." A chilling fear ran down my spine. I had never seen such desperation in his eyes. At that moment, we both knew that our survival was in question.

A few minutes later, Jim looked out the porthole window and saw that we had drifted—land was much closer than expected. There is an extensive reef along the island of Eleuthera called the "Devil's Backbone" and it was aptly named. Jim realized that we were dangerously near to it. If we crashed onto the reef, there was no telling how badly we might be injured. He turned to me and firmly said, "We have to get off the boat, now."

Jim climbed onto the bow of the boat to untie the dinghy. He looked like Spiderman as he crawled his way there on his belly with his arms and legs stretched out to keep himself balanced. I remained below to gather whatever essential gear we needed. I felt the familiar wave of nausea wash over me, but I continued prying open the cabinets to scoop up important documents, our passports, and the EPIRB. My stomach turned, and I ran up the steps just in time to vomit into the rope locker at the top of the companionway.

Jim got the dinghy into the water and dragged it to the stern of the boat. He tied a rope to a grab handle and handed me a tether to tie to the second one. The waves were slamming the dinghy against the keel of the boat as he attempted to get the outboard onto the deck and attach it to the dinghy. Jim feared that the continued battering of the dinghy against the stern might puncture it. He decided to move it to the port side of the boat where we could affix the outboard motor without the sailboat pounding down on it. When he unhooked the tether,

Sogno Mio (My Dream) lifted up and pulled away. At that same moment, the other tie line snapped, and the two boats drifted apart.

We froze, both dumbfounded as the scene unfolded. I was on Sogno Mio, and Jim was on the dinghy being pulled away by the swells. He was without a life jacket, paddles, or motor amid twenty-foot seas. He was ten to fifteen feet away in mere seconds. All I could think was that this was the end; we would literally drift apart and never see each other again. He couldn't jump in the shark infested waters. I was terrified; I was sure that we would both die apart from each other. Then he snapped out of it. With no oars to aid him, he paddled with both hands and yelled for me to throw him a line. I ran to the winches to find a rope. As I went to toss him a line, the capricious sea swelled and catapulted the dingy back to the sailboat, slamming the dinghy into the port side. He grabbed the line and quickly secured it. We breathed a momentary sigh of relief; we were back together again.

Once we got our essential gear in plastic garbage bags, Jim and I took our final leave of Sogno Mio. Jim held the dinghy steady for me as I attempted to get in. He was always looking out for me, trying to take care of me, and making sure that I always had everything I needed. That has never changed, and none of that was lost on me. I looked at him, nodded, then jumped into the boat.

Jim sat with his hand on the motor, keeping watch on what was in front of us; I faced him from the bow of the dinghy and watched what was coming from behind. The waves breached the boat, but I was ready with a bucket to bail the water. It seemed like a never-ending battle, but it kept me busy. I didn't have time to worry about our safety. We had to do whatever was needed to get to shore. We were both alert and we seemed to dodge the breaking waves well enough.

We knew we couldn't go straight to shore because the Devil's Backbone stretched for miles along the coastline, the next inlet was thirty miles up the coast. We were both scared and wondered what would happen next. However, there was no room for addressing our fears; we had to forge ahead.

I'm not sure how long we were motoring, but it seemed like hours. The swells created fifteen-foot walls rising all around us. We could see land so clearly when we were at the crest of a wave. But the valley between them was ominous; walls of gray ocean seemed to push inward towards us. I was claustrophobic being surrounded by the encroaching sea, hoping that none of the waves would break and come tumbling down on us. We forged on as the sun got lower in the sky, and there was still no port in sight. Since most of the island was uninhabited, we made the decision to brave the crossing the coral reef. There were houses along the shore and figured it would be a likely place to get help.

We changed tack and headed directly toward the shore. As we got closer to the reef, the churning waters became more and more violent. Waves were crashing onto each other with greater force. The white water tossed, pushed, and pulled us in all different directions. The sound was thunderous, and we had to shout to be heard. We had made it to the Devil's Backbone, and it was time to cross over. The Devil's Backbone is a well-known coral reef off the island of Eleuthera in the Bahamas. It was infamous for causing hundreds of shipwrecks over the years. Reaching it in an eight-foot dinghy was terrifying.

We braced ourselves for the trial that lay ahead. Jim tried to time our crossing with the break of the waves. He studied them like a surfer waiting for the perfect swell at just the right moment. With little warning, he made his move. He came at it from an angle and tried to ride the top of a breaking wave. It was coming at us from behind. He tried to rev the motor to get some speed, but it wasn't powerful enough. As we crested the wave, we felt it buckle beneath us. The waves tossed the dinghy about like a leaf in the wind, and there was nothing to keep us steady. Water was coming at us from every direction, but we were still afloat. We thought we might just make it when another surge hit us from the side and crashed directly into us. It flipped us over pounding us under the surf. Everything in the dinghy went flying into the sea, including us.

It all happened in the blink of an eye. The rush of the breaking water tossed me in multiple directions. I was completely disoriented. Submerged beneath the waves, I opened my eyes and all I could see was white water swirling around me; it was coming in at me from all sides. My heart was beating rapidly; I couldn't breathe. I desperately tried to get back to the surface for air, but I couldn't tell which way was up. I could no longer see the dinghy. I thrashed about and paddled as hard as I could, trying to figure out which direction would lead me to the surface. Then I noticed the direction the bubbles were moving in and followed them. I used my upper body to propel my way up, only to find myself under the capsized dinghy.

The surf was still churning, and there were no air pockets under the dinghy. I dove down but couldn't get much distance; it felt like something was holding me back. I worked my way back up to the surface and once again came up under the dinghy. I was running out of oxygen, and I needed to get my head above the water immediately. I dove down a final time and tried to go deeper to clear the boat. I emerged with my head bouncing on the rubber pontoon, still under water. The surface was to my left or my right. I had a fifty-fifty chance of getting it right. I took a chance. Thankfully, I came up right beside the outboard motor. Gasping for air, I heard Jim frantically yelling my name; he had panicked when he didn't see me. He searched for me in vain. Diving below, he saw nothing but white water. It was so turbulent that he had trouble staying afloat without hanging on to the dinghy. After several failed attempts, he just held on and shouted for me. When he finally saw me, he cried out with relief.

"Oh my God, Mario, I thought you were gone! Are you all right? Just hang on."

When I could finally speak, I responded, "I think so, just trying to catch my breath."

Jim instructed, "Mario, get on the wave side of the dinghy so it can push us toward the shore." But I wiggled around in a frenzy. Something was wrong.

"Jim, I can't move my legs. I don't know what's happening!"

"Do you have any pain? Can you feel them?"

"No pain, I can move my feet. It feels like something is strangling me."

As I thrashed, I realized that the ropes and gas line were tangled around my legs and waist. I couldn't break free. When we capsized, the lines got caught in the motor's propeller, wrapped around my legs, and pulled tight. I was trapped. That is why I had so much trouble getting up to the surface when we were thrown overboard. Besides being tethered to the dinghy motor, I could only use my arms to swim. With the raging waters pushing me in all directions, it was a losing battle. I gasped for air as the swells continued to break over me. I was having trouble catching my breath through each hit from the crashing waves. Thankfully, with Jim's help, I finally broke free of the lines.

Both Jim and I were in shock; the reality of what we had just survived began to sink in. We had been pounded into the reef under the tumultuous waters. The surf slammed our bodies against the rocks and dead coral, like rag dolls. Had it not been for our foul weather gear, we would have suffered serious lacerations. There was only a moment to absorb the fact that we had survived with minor injuries. But it wasn't over yet. The shoreline was still several miles away.

We hung on to the dinghy and gradually calmed down. We knew that we had to think rationally to survive. There were roughly two miles to go before we reached the shore. We hoped that the waves would eventually push us further into land.

Firm in our resolve, we kicked our legs and pushed the dinghy toward shore. We were still in the middle of the reef and were surrounded by white water. It got quiet for a long time; the only sound was from the crashing waves. To keep alert, I focused on a house that was particularly grand and beautiful. I concentrated on making it there. Meanwhile, Jim saw dark shadows beneath him, and his fear mounted. Aggressive sharks were swimming around Sogno Mio when we abandoned her. We were not more than a mile away from there. Could there be sharks near us? Everything was a blur as we floated above the ominous dark images. He kept his eyes focused below and scanned the waters to spot any of those shadows coming closer. He thought, "Damn it! What do we do if they come after us? I wonder if they'll attack if we're just swimming by?"

We were both so fatigued and desperate to be on shore. I didn't know how much longer I could keep it up. That house seemed much closer than it actually was. Then we heard the blades of the Coast Guard helicopter roar above us. We were beyond relieved. We turned and waved to signal them, but they passed right by us. It made little sense; we had the EPIRB with us and were certain that they had gotten a lock on its signal. They missed us even though we were wearing our bright yellow foul weather gear. However, the strong winds and the high seas created whitecaps on the waves made it extremely difficult for them to see us. We both felt a bit desperate in that moment. It looked like they were heading toward the abandoned boat. We just hoped that they would circle around to rescue us.

As time passed, we were both growing weaker. Amidst the sound of the waves and the surf, we continued checking in with one another to make sure we were alert. After so much time submerged in the sea, our body temperatures were getting lower, and we began to shiver. We had been in the water for hours. Finally, we looked up and saw we were only about fifty feet from the shore. At that moment, we heard the helicopter once again, and we waved; it was the Coast Guard at last. They flew in a circle and tried to land on the beach.

Suddenly, the beach was filled with people. They had finally come out of their houses and gathered around us. The helicopter hovered above at the other end of the beach and dropped a line. Down came several young Coast Guard officers in dark blue jumpsuits. To our dismay, once they were convinced that we weren't seriously injured, and when we were safely on land, they ran off to board the helicopter. They had used up so much fuel searching for us that they couldn't take us on board.

Seeing my panic, a man in the crowd reached out to me. "Hi, my name is Ralph. I assure you we'll take good care of you. Don't worry about getting back home right now. We need to get you warm and dry."

The next thing I recall is that I was in a hot shower, away from all the inquiring people and chaos on the shore. The scene on the beach was a blur to me. I couldn't process all that had happened during the last few hours. The stream of heat from the shower head felt like a balm on my battered flesh. I felt dizzy and had to steady myself against the walls of the shower. Having been on the boat or in the water for days, my legs felt wobbly on land. Soon, my whole body shook—the reality of what we had just survived sank in. We had been in peril, and our lives had been in great jeopardy. Tears mingled with the warm spray on my face, and soon my entire body convulsed as I cried. My anxiety slowly drained away as the hot water warmed my body.

We were safe; the trauma was over, and we still had each other. That was all that mattered.

WHY?

I think back on that saga so many years ago. The usual questions pop into my mind. What was the meaning of those struggles? Why did so many things go wrong at once? Was there some sort of message or lesson that we were supposed to learn as a result?

My time in the Caribbean remains one of the most significant turning points in my life. Who I was before that tumultuous year was very different from the man who emerged from that trauma. The emotional crisis that caused me to flee from my life in California led me to re-evaluate the meaning of my life after our experience. Finding meaning in what took place during our painful sailing adventures has taken years. After sailing in one direction for so many decades, I believe that I have come about, changed directions.

So, what's the point? Why did I include this in my reflections on grief? I used to believe that God placed trials in our lives to teach us some sort of lesson or help us to grow stronger. That's what I was taught in my Catholic school. But I don't believe that any longer. It seems to me that a higher power that purposely inflicts pain on people would be quite cruel. One of my least favorite phrases people use when trying to console others is, "It's God's will." If a person believes in a loving God, it would be incongruous to think that God would cause suffering just to teach a lesson. That is counter to all I learned in my theological studies.

The trials and tribulations of life are simply part of the human experience. We experience pain and struggles, but we also celebrate life's joys. As the years have gone by, I realize that it's up to me to extract meaning from life's experiences. Only then will I be able to move on from the pain. I don't believe that things happen for a reason. I believe it's up to us to reflect on what happens and then give it meaning. I know that it is up to me to learn from all that happens in my life, from my failures and my successes.

Many of us struggled with disappointment throughout our lives. Each circumstance and experience is an opportunity for learning and growth. Some of those experiences are more challenging than others, and only we, as individuals can find meaning in them. If I had chosen to wallow in my sadness, I would have sunk deeper into that pain. That would have made it all the more difficult to move on and become a stronger person.

There was one stark realization for me. I know now that, no matter how much I love Jim or how much he loves me, each of us had to take care of ourselves. There were many circumstances when we had to find our own strength and resilience: we weren't always able to rely on each other for rescue. I had to use my own knowledge and strength to find a solution. I remember the moment the lines snapped when Jim and I went to recover Sogno Mio. I knew that he might drift far away from me on that dinghy in the stormy sea without a life jacket. I was left stranded on the sailboat that was headed on a collision course with the coral reef. At that moment, there was nothing either of us could do but rely upon our individual intellect and strength. I couldn't give up and cry. I had to think fast and make choices. I had to draw from my own well of knowledge and make calculated decisions.

When I was trapped under the dinghy, Jim wasn't there to protect me. I had to figure it out for myself. I had to use my fortitude and stamina to claw my way to the surface. I couldn't rely upon anyone else at that moment; I had to tap into the power and knowledge within me to get through. The more prepared I was regarding boats and sailing, the more likely I would be to survive and thereby help Jim. The same held true for him. People can only help others if they are strong enough to help themselves. I suppose it's like the airplane announcement says: You need to put on your own air mask before helping those around you. For me, that remains one of the most difficult lessons I learned.

My perspective on life was transformed during the years following our trauma. I found it difficult to move beyond my disappointment at losing all we had hoped for our future as well as our savings. The dream of life in the Caribbean was crushed under the waves that nearly drowned us. Always one to search for deeper meaning, I tread water trying to understand why it all happened. Why did we survive? I didn't know how to navigate the unfamiliar waters of a forty-year-old man trying to re-create his life after losing everything. We were living in the basement of my parents' home. I had no job and therefore, I had no identity.

I was lost and I was angry. Was I angry at God? Did I even believe in God anymore? Try as I might, I could not find meaning in that harrowing sailing adventure. But I had to move on, find a job, and get on with life. I learned to bury the grief under the practical necessities of life. Buried grief is different from repressed grief in that one knows it's there. There is a conscious effort to place it out of one's mind. The effects can manifest themselves in similar ways: unfocused sadness, anger, or depression.

But I discovered a way to cope. I focused my energies on positive or productive activities. I found a teaching position at Marymount School, a Catholic school for girls in New York City. I taught music to girls from fourth to twelfth grades. I threw myself into my work as I built another music program. I grew the choir to over eighty singers and traveled throughout Europe on concert tours. My identity was integrally intertwined with my role of teacher and music director. Being creative helped me climb out of that traumatic experience at sea. Marymount was a loving and supportive community that helped me regain my sense of self-worth and identity.

Grief, I've learned, is really just love.
It's all the love you want to give, but cannot.
All of that unspent love gathers in the corners of your eyes, the lump in your throat,
and in the hollow part of your chest.
Grief is just love with no place to go.

—Jamie Anderson

11
PARKINSON'S

Following our Caribbean adventure, we moved to New York. My parents lived with me and my husband toward my father's final years. During that time, Dad was diagnosed with Parkinson's disease. He was frustrated and resentful. Why did he suffer from a disease that no one in his family had ever had? Dad was disheartened by his steady decline. Each loss of ability or motor function was a blow to his dignity. He was a fiercely proud man. I recall walking by his bedroom as he did sit-ups to keep his stomach flat. He was over eighty at the time. He always shaved, put on cologne, and dressed well. He took pride in his looks and how he presented himself. Quiet and reserved with family members, Dad was loquacious with neighbors and friends. He bragged about his children's accomplishments and told stories of the old country. He reveled in regaling an audience with tales of life in Italy. As Parkinson's deteriorated his speech, he became discouraged when he could not communicate well. Daily walks to the market or church became less frequent as his agility decreased.

My mother, Tina never left his side, and they continued to do minor chores around the house to keep engaged and active. Staying busy distracted him from his plight and feeling useful helped his ego. During one of their ordinary tasks, his life took a tragic turn. They had just washed and dried the laundry in the kitchen. Tina handed each folded item to Larry, and he dutifully placed it into the basket. When they were done, she went down to the basement to put the other load into the dryer. Larry, wanting to be helpful, decided to bring the basket of clothes up to the second floor. He bent over and lifted the basket without a struggle, walked carefully to the staircase, and began to ascend one step at a time. But the weight of the basket caused him to lose his balance. He tried desperately to correct himself, but it was of no use. He let go of the clothes and reached out for the banister rail and missed. Larry fell backward down the stairs onto the wooden floor. He barely felt his body hit the floor when his head hit the brass hinges on the closet door, causing him to see stars. A flash of pain shot through his body and knocked him out.

Tina heard the commotion and flew into the foyer to see what had happened. There he was, lying on the floor with blood streaming from his head. She screamed.

"Larry, Larry. Oh, my God! What did you do?"

There was no response. Tina ran to the phone and dialed 911. Kneeling by his side, she patted down his hair and caressed his face.

"It's going to be okay, my love. Help is coming. Don't worry. I've got you, amore. I've got you."

Tina couldn't stop her tears as he lay in a pool of blood, unresponsive.

"Please be okay, Larry. I love you. Please, please."

Slowly, he regained consciousness but was disoriented. He wanted to be helped up, so Tina helped him sit upright, leaning against the door. Sitting in his own blood rattled him. The sight of it made him queasy. Tina knew he was getting more anxious.

"Don't move, Larry. Just stay still. I'll get some rags to clean this up."

She ran into the kitchen, returning with a pile of rags, and mopped up as much as possible.

"The ambulance is on its way, Larry. It won't be long."

The words were barely out of her mouth when they heard the siren and saw the flashing lights. Tina opened the door, and paramedics wheeled a stretcher into the house. The rest of the afternoon was a blur to her.

Jim and I took the commuter train home from the city and sat with him in a packed emergency room. It was a Friday, and the place was bustling, which made it difficult for Larry to rest. His speech was labored.

"I...I'm thirsty," he choked out.

"Sorry, sir," the nurse responded. "We can't give you water. You may need surgery."

It was late in the evening; after spending nine hours in the emergency room, they admitted him to the intensive care unit. The swelling of his brain from the impact of the fall caused them to worry. The doctors were unclear about his prognosis but told the family to get his affairs in order. By that time, all his children were by his side. For the following week, Larry drifted in and out of consciousness. They drained the fluid from his brain, which relieved some pressure, but he was still in danger.

"Larry is incredibly strong," the doctor told the family. "I have never seen anyone fight as hard as he has."

"Will he recover, Doctor?" Tina asked.

"To be honest, I didn't think he would make it," she responded. "He is stable for now. But I need you to understand he may never be back to what he was before. You need to prepare yourself."

After two weeks, he was moved to a local rehabilitation center. However, his faculties were never the same. He began to hallucinate and could not understand why Tina was abandoning him when visiting hours were over.

"Where you go?" he asked in his thick Italian accent.

"Larry, I have to go home. I'll be back tomorrow."

"I come with you," he insisted as he tried to get out of bed. But he was strapped into the bed to prevent him from falling. When he realized that, his eyes grew wide and his paranoia kicked in. He believed he was being held prisoner.

"Larry, I can't stay. I promise I will be back first thing in the morning."

"No, I come home with you."

It broke Tina's heart. He could not understand where he was and that she could not stay overnight. It was bad enough that he experienced so much physical pain, but the lack of cognition was much worse. Each night, it was the same thing. He was relentless and made her feel as if she was abandoning him. For two months, she suffered the same routine.

The most sacred time for Larry had always been with his children gathered around the dinner table. He sat back and took it all in—the pandemonium of several conversations at once, food being passed around the table, and the laughter of people who were entirely too familiar with one another. As dishes were cleared, he would often catch the ear of whoever sat beside him. That was when he shone, telling stories of his childhood and life back in Bisceglie, Italy. His tales were often a bit more fantastic than real, but that's what made them great stories. When Tina came back to the table, she would chime in, and his yarn would become ever longer.

That Thanksgiving, his absence was palpable. Once the table was cleared and the dishes washed, my sisters took their turn visiting Larry with their spouses and children. Later in the evening, my brother and Tina returned for the final visit. They all hoped that Larry would be home for Christmas, and their wish came to pass. On December 23, the day before Christmas Eve, 2008, he was released from rehab and came home to White Plains.

It was clear from the moment he entered the house that his life with me and Jim would be drastically different. Although he was significantly impaired, Larry's memory led him to follow his routine. The master bedroom was on the second floor, but he could not manage the stairs any longer. A gate had to be placed at the top of the stairs so he wouldn't try to descend on his own. They considered setting up a bed on the first floor, but there was no shower in the tiny powder room off the dining room. And although we hoped that our lives would return to normal upon returning, that was far from reality. Dad had a faraway look in his eyes and had great difficulty speaking. It broke our hearts, but he and Mom tried to carry on as they had before the fall.

I was the choir director at Marymount, an all-girls school in Manhattan. On Christmas Eve, six of my singers traveled from the city to welcome my father home. Both Larry and Tina had attended their choral concerts in New York City, and the girls had a great affection for them. My singers gathered around the piano with Larry and Tina sitting before them. They intoned the first song, and one of the girls said, "Since you couldn't come to our Christmas concert this year, we thought we'd come to you."

Mom and I were overwhelmed by their thoughtfulness. Larry sat in the overstuffed chair with Tina at his side. He was still disoriented since his return home and wore a blank face with a distant look in his eyes. But once the girls began to sing, he perked up and turned his head in their direction. Noticing the change in his demeanor, my heart swelled. He was thrilled to have these lovely young women before them. As they began to sing, tears welled in his eyes. It was the most beautiful gift they could have offered.

The months that followed were difficult. Although Dad continued to heal and grow stronger, he was not himself—it was as if a part of him was missing. He was not able to speak in full sentences, and it was difficult to understand him. There was a great deal of guesswork involved when conversing with him. As the months passed and winter turned to spring and summer, Tina encouraged Larry to walk down the street with her to get a bit of exercise, but Larry became fearful of losing his way.

He became more and more paranoid. Reasoning with him wasn't helpful. He was suspicious of everything. One evening, Larry went to the bathroom, and hearing the voices on the television, he believed that people had come into the house. He was afraid to come out in his pajamas for fear that he wasn't appropriately dressed. The distinction between reality and the world of television blurred. He thought the characters were real and were watching him. He began hallucinating, believing that people in the backyard were threatening to come into the house.

He also had many lucid moments. Larry had always been a handsome man, and he took care to dress in slacks and button-down shirts. On several occasions, college friends of mine visited. Larry disappeared, returning with the smell of Old Spice aftershave. He always took special care with how he looked. However, his dexterity had deteriorated, and he had trouble managing his buttons or belt. Nonetheless, Larry insisted on dressing up. Tina helped him dress and encouraged him to wear suspenders, because he could no longer buckle his belt.

"No, I don't want to wear this shit," he declared as they were running off to a doctor's appointment. "Give me the belt."

"Larry, we're going to be late. Come on now. Just wear the suspenders. They are so much easier for you."

"No, no! They look terrible," he said as he fumbled with the belt.

Tina began to cry in frustration. The physical and emotional burden of caring for him had steadily broken her down.

"Why can't you just listen to me, Larry? You make things more difficult. We are going to be late," she said through her tears.

He was startled by her reaction and froze. What have I done? He knew she was just trying to help. She was his rock. The last thing he wanted to do was hurt her. Larry let the belt drop to the floor, shuffled over to her, and took her in his arms.

"Tina, I'm sorry."

It was the first step of many in giving up control. As the months passed, his mental and physical health deteriorated even more. Home health aides came twice a week to help Tina care for him. The aide bathed and dressed him and led him through physical therapy. Mom joined in, and they would do the exercises together.

Thanksgiving rolled back around, and the family was grateful to have Larry at the table with them. Just a year before, they had taken turns visiting him at the rehabilitation center. This time, he took his place at the head of the table with Tina by his side. The usual chaos of dinner gave the holiday a festive air despite Larry's distance. Speaking was difficult for him, and he seemed detached from conversations and the jovial interaction taking place all around him. Still, his family was comforted by the fact that Larry was right where he should be. They rested in the knowledge that even though he couldn't participate as he normally would, Larry was at the table with his loving family.

Christmas was a blur that year as Larry receded further from the world. Family gatherings found him entirely disengaged and barely eating. One would have to sit directly in front of him to get his attention and call his name. Walking became more difficult; he didn't have the strength to get from his chair to the bed. My brother-in-law, David, would lift him up and carry him to bed. He had lost so much weight that he felt like a child in David's arms.

As the Parkinson's continued to worsen, their days were busy with practical tasks like dressing, eating, and bathing. Tina didn't know how much Larry understood regarding his condition. Does he realize how bad it is? she wondered. They never discussed it, nor did they consider that he could be nearing the end of his battle. Tina couldn't let herself ponder the inevitable.

One snowy day, my school was closed, and Dad was at the kitchen table. Mom was frustrated with Larry.

"Larry, you have to eat something. Please, have a little soup."

He turned his head away from the spoon she held up to his lips.

"Ugh! At least try. What is wrong with you? You need to eat!" She was exasperated.

"Mom, let him be. Don't force him," I said gently.

"Look at him. He's losing so much weight. I don't know what to do anymore."

Mom walked away, visibly upset—at her wit's end. Emotionally and physically drained, she was only beginning to come to terms with his deteriorating condition. Tina could tell he was nearing his end, but she could not face it. She focused

solely on his recovery. I sat at the table with Dad and put my hand on top of his. At my touch, Dad was pulled from his distant gaze and looked up at me.

"Dad, what's the matter? Are you not hungry?"

He shook his head.

"How about a little water? I'm sure you're dehydrated."

He shook his head once again.

"It's okay, Pop. You don't have to do anything you don't want to. No one is going to force you to eat or drink, all right?"

Larry nodded his head. I turned to see my mother watching our encounter with tears in her eyes. We knew what this meant. I brought Mom to the other room and sat her down.

"Mom, I know it's frustrating, but you can't make him do anything he doesn't want to."

"But if he doesn't eat or drink, he'll waste away. I can see it happening already." A single tear trickled down her cheek.

"I know, Mom." There was silence, and then I continued, "But he has to do this his own way. He's taking back control. It's the only power he has left."

Mom shook her head. "I'm standing by watching him leave me, and there is nothing I can do."

I pulled her close to me and said, "You can love him, Mom, as you always have. Just be with him, hold him, and tell him you love him."

Silence engulfed us as the gravity of the moment weigh upon our heavy hearts. Later, I helped my father to the couch and tried to reinforce the fact that he was in charge of his own destiny.

"Pop, you do what you need to do. You've had an awful year, and I know this is torture for you. You know we'll all be okay, right? We'll take care of Mom. I promise."

Larry looked into my eyes, and although he could

no longer formulate full words or sentences, he managed to stammer, "I...I... love..."

"I love you too, Dad, more than you know."

With tears falling from my eyes, I could barely see the snowy roads as I drove that day. I was not more than a mile away from their house when I lost control of the car and skidded over the curb, stopping just feet before a towering tree. My body shook with the shock of what nearly happened. I rested my forehead on the steering wheel and cried.

From then on, my father stopped eating and drinking. He refused to take his medication, and he became weaker by the hour. Five days later, Dad had trouble breathing. The hospice nurse arrived shortly after and stayed throughout the night. When Dad's breathing grew more labored, the nurse turned to Mom and said, "This is what they call the death rattle. It won't be long now."

My mother took her place beside him in the narrow hospital bed and held him in her arms. She could tell he was in pain, so the nurse increased the morphine drip, giving him a small dose every thirty minutes. Tina was beside him, holding his hand when he breathed his last breath. All at once, the room became quiet. The death rattle had ceased—Larry labored no more. The doctor came just before dawn to pronounce him dead. It was February 17, 2010, on Ash Wednesday.

LOSING DAD

I watched my father's steady decline for years, but after his fall, it was a precipitous descent. Dad was frustrated with his declining autonomy and inability to communicate his needs. He was conscious of each loss and suffered both physically as well as emotionally. In his final months, I watched as he became more distant. He retreated from our world. It was a painful journey for him and for each of my siblings and mother.

At some point, I looked toward his death as a relief from his suffering. The evolution of my emotions and attitude toward Dad was unconscious. No longer was it a matter of fighting to keep him alive or help him to recover. Not knowing when it occurred, the family transitioned to anticipatory grief. For me, it was as bad as death. Each moment was filled with the fear of its inevitability while at the same time welcoming death to end his suffering. His impending passing was certain. But the months of steady decline felt as if the loss of life was with us every day. It was a darkness that cast a shadow over us until the end.

I didn't realize how much the darkness colored my life. Once my father died, I experienced the pain of losing a parent. It was a different kind of pain than I had ever experienced. I turned inward, shying away from large gatherings of friends or family. Being the center of attention gave me great anxiety. This posed a significant problem since I am a choir conductor. The spotlight was always on me and my choirs. I was always speaking to large audiences. I was an entertainer. But after Dad passed, I eschewed that role. I was reluctant to laugh and socialize. Somehow, it seemed to be a betrayal of my loss.

As the months and years passed, the shroud of grief lifted. I believed Dad was with us, that his spirit continued to watch over us. I found comfort in sharing stories about him and imitating his strong Italian accent. Tales of his idiosyncrasies brought laughter to our table and allowed us to celebrate his life. In the months that followed his passing, my siblings and I focused on caring for our grieving mother. All our focus was now on her. She was alive and was suffering the loss of her soulmate. We were determined to bring joy back into her life. My grief was transformed into caring for Mom.

The reality is that you will grieve forever.
You will not 'get over' the loss of a loved one;
You will learn to live with it.
You will heal and you will rebuild yourself
around the loss you have suffered.
You will be whole again but you will never be the same.
Nor should you be the same
Nor would you want to.

—Elisabeth Kübler-Ross

12
ANTICIPATION

During the last two years of my mother's life, I experience an unfamiliar fear. It was with me each and every hour of the day. I couldn't shake the feeling of dread at every phone call or text from my sister. Each time I visited my mother, I feared it would be my last. It began slowly as her declining health eclipsed the vivacious personality I had always known. Her boundless energy and ceaseless storytelling trickled away. Rather than life, I saw the anticipation of death. She spoke more of her ailments and of seeing my father again. Her face belied the suffering in her aging body. Gone was the joy of living and spending time with us. My heart ached at seeing her pain and I knew what lay ahead. For nearly two years, the anticipatory grief over losing her was excruciating.

Mom lived more than thirteen years after Dad's passing. Her death was no surprise. She was ninety-two years old. Tina lived a full and happy life, but it was not without struggle. Orphaned during the Second World War, Tina experienced loss early in her life. Her mother died when Tina was only seven years old. Her father was working in a foreign land at the time and died a few years later. Coming from a family of relative wealth, she then experienced the loss of that wealth and status in addition to the loss of her parents. However, Tina was a dreamer and an optimist. She embraced life and created a world of love. She gathered all those in her orbit who would join her. She told detailed stories of growing up in southern Italy, painting images of a bustling fishing village rife with drama. She gathered her family around the dinner table and fed us with culture and history. Although there was no formal ceremony to suppertime, the ritual of gathering to share a meal grounded her family. Even as we grew older and left home, reuniting at Sunday dinners kept us connected.

I was fortunate to spend a great deal of time with her in my adult years. At some point after my father passed, Mom handed me a stack of love letters she and my father had written over sixty years before. My three siblings and I were raised hearing the stories of their clandestine love affair through the written word. Having recently emigrated from the same hometown in Italy, my father had seen a photograph of my mother enclosed in a letter from his brother. What ensued was two years of letter writing and a proposal of marriage. But they promised each other that if the intensity of their passion expressed in the written word was absent upon meeting, they would part as friends.

Holding their letters in my hands, I met my mother's eyes. I knew what must be done.

"Mom, why don't you read them to me? It would mean so much more to hear your voice reading the words of your eighteen-year-old self."

With each letter, a world an ocean away and decades before came alive in vivid detail. I could see Mom transported to her teenage self, with all the anxiety and drama of youth on full display. Their letters sparked memories long forgotten. She painted their history as tangent upon tangent led her through their ordinary lives in cinematic splendor. I was riveted by her retelling of stories I had heard many times before. They came alive in ways I never anticipated. I learned who Tina and Larry were as young people in love. Mom described their longing and their dreams, their fears and insecurities. I came to know Tina and Larry as characters in the story of their lives. For the first time, I became friends with two young lovers who were not simply my mom and dad.

Over four years, Mom and I read through those letters. Each time we sat at the table more questions came to mind. Tina's candor was remarkable. She held nothing back. It wasn't a fantasy romance, but rather a story of real people trying to make their way in a complicated world. I decided to write a book framed by those letters. I was compelled to share their love story. The youngest of four children, I was very connected to my mother. I had always had an emotionally intimate relationship with her. I never dreamed that we would be drawn even closer together through the writing of that book. The hours, days, weeks, and years spent writing *Letters from Italy* tethered our hearts. She let me into her life in ways I never imagined.

Once *Letters from Italy* was published, Mom became the greatest of marketers. During the final year of her life, she must have prompted the sale of hundreds of copies. She was so proud of it, she mentioned it to each healthcare worker that came by. She shared vignettes of her life and proudly displayed her copy. Many sought her signature after purchasing a copy, even during the final week of her life. I am incredibly grateful that we shared that experience before she became ill. The book was published just after she turned ninety years old.

THE FALL

A year after the book came out, I got a job offer in Northern California. Many years before, my husband and I lived in San Francisco for over a decade, and we longed to return. I am a choral director and have created and/or developed thriving programs throughout my life. Choral positions rarely arise, and I feared if I let this opportunity pass by, I might not get another chance. I was excited to explore one more opportunity to make music back in California. However, it would mean leaving Mom during the last years of her life. I labored over the decision.

I dreaded telling Mom. We both knew what that meant. I would no longer be able to drop in and spend the afternoon with her. We wouldn't be able to prepare the traditional Christmas Eve feast of the seven fishes. We wouldn't be frying meatballs and making the Sunday sauce. Yes, we would have phone calls and FaceTime. I would visit, yet our ordinary time together would be scarce. But Mom was never one to get in the way of her children's dreams. She wanted nothing more than to see them thrive, embark on new adventures, and launch them into the world. Ultimately, I knew she would be happy for me.

My husband, Jim, and I hosted one last family barbecue at our home in White Plains, New York. The family recounted the many holidays celebrated at our home. It was tinged with melancholy. We understood that eighteen years of family gatherings at our home had come to an end. Even so, there was the promise of new experiences living in the wine country of Sonoma County.

A few weeks later, just before our departure, Mom rose in the middle of the night to use the restroom. With sleep in her eyes, she lost her balance and fell. She landed face down on the floor. Her nose hit first, and her head snapped back. Dazed, she lay there trying to regain her bearings and let the pain subside. Eventually, she garnered enough strength to lift herself up and into bed. The following day, in addition to the black eye and bruised nose, her neck ached. My sister, Marisa brought her to the emergency room at St. Vincent's Hospital. Mom had fractured her nose and neck. Not only was she in physical pain, but it seemed that the light, which had always lit her path with optimism had dimmed. Tina was discouraged and frustrated.

My siblings and I worried that her fall would lead to a rapid decline. Not since my father died had we seen her spirit so low. With only a week until our departure for California, I was beside myself. How could I leave Mom in this condition? I realized there was likely little time left for her and that I would be very far away. Regret over my decision to leave crept in, but there was nothing I could do. Our house was sold, and I had resigned from my teaching position. The wheels were in motion and there was no way to stop them.

Jim and I had packed up our house in New York and planned to stay at Marisa's house for a day before driving to California. My heart ached at seeing Mom in such a state. The prospect of leaving her was fraught with regret. How could I possibly leave her now? What kind of son leaves his mother when she needs him the most? My heart ached. The hours we spent together we're tender. We were all hopeful that in a few months, Mom would be free of the neck brace and on the mend. We spoke of the new adventure that lay ahead for us in California. Mom was as upbeat as she possibly could be. But the following day, when the hour of departure drew near, I could see her eyes grow dark. Her lips trembled. I took her hand.

"Mom, what's wrong?"

"She knows you'll be leaving soon, and she's upset," my sister said.

"Oh, Mom. You know this story so well. You left everyone you loved back in Italy when you married Dad. And look at the incredible life you created for us."

"I know, Mario. I know. But I will miss you so very much."

My heart, already breaking, felt heavy in my chest. I thought it was a cruel twist of fate that she should hurt herself so badly just as we were leaving. I promised to visit during the holidays, and I told her I would FaceTime every Saturday. All of us looked to the prospect of her healing getting back to normal. But that wasn't to be the case.

At ninety-one years of age, her bones were not healing. Rather than grow together, the fracture had become worse. She was told that she would have to wear a neck brace for the rest of her life. It seemed a bitter final chapter of a life well lived. She suffered its discomfort more than the actual pain. She found it difficult to read, which was one of her passions. It caused her to sweat and dig into the back of her head. It had been many years since she slept through a night and now it had become even more arduous. A year of wearing the brace wore her down. We could see her joy and zest for life beginning to wane. She spoke more and more about joining my father in heaven.

She fell several more times after the initial break, and each fall weakened her further. She suffered a significant bout of pneumonia and congestive heart failure. Both events prompted what I call goodbye conversations. I traveled for a visit just after Christmas to celebrate the family's winter birthdays. Mom was frail and in physical distress on my birthday. I left the family at the dining room table and stole away to spend time in her room. It was early January. The new year found her a year older and weaker. Her mind and body told her that this would be the year of her death. I knelt at her feet as she sat in her recliner. Her voice was faint, and her breathing labored. She took my hands in hers and looked into my eyes.

"Mario, I want you to know how much I love you. You are a good man and so talented. You have done so many wonderful things. I need you to believe in your goodness. You are good just the way you are. You have given so much of your life to others. You must understand how many people you have touched, and you continue to do so. I love you."

I knew what she was doing—telling me, her gay son, that I was good and loved just the way I was. Over the years, she and I had many conversations about being gay in the Catholic Church. Time and again, she expressed her dismay with official Catholic teaching that condemned homosexual behavior. "Can't they understand how powerful love is? What does it matter who you love? When you find the right person, it transforms you."

Tina was a woman beyond her time. She always was.

During the last nine months of her life, Mom approached each day with as much positive thinking as she could muster. Sleepless nights were the norm, followed by days trying to stay awake but nodding off in her chair. Although she desperately wanted to attend Mass, my sisters feared the spread of Covid. So, Mom contented herself with watching the Mass on television each day, followed by the rosary. Although she often fell asleep during the rosary, this ritual kept Mom centered. It gave her the strength she needed to get through another day.

ON EDGE

I visited home six times during her last year. Four months before she died, Mom was in rare form talking about the future, making plans for the holidays, and ordering us all around. As the matriarch of the family, she had that right, and she did it well. She relished time with her great-grandchildren and although cooking a full meal was much too strenuous, she enjoyed having her hand in the preparations as she instructed Marisa and me at each turn. The neck brace was a constant burden, especially during the summer months. She could never handle extreme heat and humidity. The brace felt like she was wearing a turtleneck in July. But she forged on and approached life with new found vigor.

Shortly after one of my visits, she fell again. The pain in her neck and back was debilitating. Gone was her positive outlook. It seemed that her physical health spiraled. Each day, I called Marisa to get updates. I realized that I was on edge, anticipating her death. I was so fearful of that day. I checked my phone each morning as soon as I woke dreading the inevitable. I hated seeing her suffer. Mom's quality of life had declined significantly. She returned to the hospital in August with congestive heart failure. It was the first week of school, but I flew back to be with her.

I had just finished narrating the book I wrote about her and my father. I sat in the hospital room watching her listen to her life story narrated by her youngest son. The smile on her face gave me such joy amidst my worry. I had done something good for Mom, a modest gift for all she had given to me over my life. When she was released from the hospital, she chose to go into hospice care. She had no desire to return to the hospital. She was done with all that. From that moment, I felt more on edge than any other time during her decline.

The morning of her death, I received a call from my brother Franco telling me that Mom had taken a turn for the worse. He was making plans to fly up to Connecticut from Florida. Being the only child of four that was not retired, I became increasingly anxious. I had just taken a week off five weeks earlier when she went into the hospital. I didn't feel good about being away from work so soon after. Knowing how uncertain her condition was, I emailed the head of school and created lesson plans for classes during my absence. I wasn't sure when I should fly back east. Should I wait until the weekend or go immediately? That's the strange thing about the end of life. No one is ever sure when death will ultimately come. She could have days, or weeks or months.

An hour later my brother called. He was crying and told me that Mom had died. I burst into tears, sobbing. An anguished groan rose from deep in my soul. I couldn't control it. My mother was gone.

Grief is like living two lives.
One is where you "pretend" everything is alright,
and the other is where your
heart silently screams in pain.

—Clearissa Lynn Castaneda

13
THE KITCHEN

The months that followed Mom's passing are a blur to me now. I started back at school immediately and had to prepare for the winter concert. As music director at a local church, I planned Christmas services and choral music for the choir. My psychic energy depleted, and I did my best to channel all I had into the tasks at hand. During the rare moments of silence, I became sullen. Upon waking each morning, the reality of her death was a lead weight preventing me from rising. I couldn't muster the strength to start another day of meaningless tasks. The emotional toll of it seeped into my physical exhaustion. My body was a collection of sandbags difficult to lift and drag along from place to place. I was subsisting. I barely had the energy to get by.

I dreaded the Christmas holidays without my mother. I couldn't bear the idea of traveling back to Connecticut knowing she would not be there for our holiday traditions. I desperately longed to feel her presence but continued to come up empty.

One of my favorite routines was preparing a seafood meal on Christmas Eve. Often called the Feast of the Seven Fishes, many Italian families cook various fish and seafood for Christmas Eve. The tradition stems from the Catholic teaching of refraining from meat on Christmas Eve.

For years, my mother, my husband Jim, and I spent hours in the kitchen preparing our Christmas Eve feast. The days before, we traveled to various markets to purchase the necessary ingredients. Arthur Avenue in the Bronx was the closest "Little Italy" to our home. A pilgrimage to each of the shops was a necessity—the butcher, the seafood store, the cheese shop, and of course, the bakery for fresh bread.

The hours we spent together passed in the blink of an eye. But the treasured moments were filled with Mom sharing her cooking expertise and stories from her childhood back in Bisceglie, Italy. She recounted encounters with her mother and father, and her beloved brother, Piero. The outdoor fish market came alive in her descriptions of southern Italy. Together, the three of us traveled back in time to a world and an ocean away. Christmas Eve was always more special to me than Christmas Day. The solemnity of the detailed preparation and execution of each course sparkled with magic and mystery. Multi-colored lights twinkling on the tree and candelabras aflame on the table imbued our celebration with sacred importance. The family was united as we carried on a tradition passed on for generations.

I desperately needed to recapture that sacred feeling. Although I was loath to attend festive holiday parties, an idea took shape. Jim and I invited a small group of friends to our table. He and I planned a meal with seven different fish or seafood. We spent days in our preparation. I set the table with our finest china and created a holiday flower arrangement. We spent hours in the kitchen cooking, and without realizing it, I felt my mother's spirit for the first time since she passed away. It was in cooking her recipes and recreating our tradition that she came alive in my heart. Although I am not a pious man, I can't help but recall the scriptural passage on the road to Emmaus. It is written that after Jesus died, two of his apostles met him on their journey to Emmaus, but they did not know who he was. It was only after they had sat for a meal together that "they recognized him in the breaking of the bread."

I needed to recreate this significant ritual. My heart demanded it. There was no expectation that I would feel Mom's presence. I wanted to do something special for us when she was alive. The day and evening were imbued with a solemnity I didn't anticipate. I met my mother in every ingredient, in the sauce I made, in the frying of the calamari. She was in my hands as I drained the pasta, in my tears as I chopped the onions, and on my tongue as I tasted the delicious food.

During the months that followed, Whenever I missed my mother so much that I could feel the pain, I pulled out my saucepan, chopped garlic, and prepared one of her meals. Week after week, I fried meatballs, and zucchini patties, and made her Sunday sauce. It was in the kitchen that we met and created traditions. If I can't feel my mother in my dreams or mind, I know I can feel her when I cook. Perhaps that is a way to feel the presence of those we love after they've passed. By following the traditions we celebrated together, I created a ritual of remembering. Each step brought me closer to my mother. I immersed myself in the sights, sounds, and aromas of her food. My senses were ignited with memories of sacred moments spent with her. The ritual of cooking has become an essential element in my grieving process.

I was dragged into a new chapter that day.
One that started when your life ended.
I grabbed at the previous pages
But life ripped them away.
New chapters have come
And many of them good.
But I still find myself
Wanting to go back.
To stay with you.
Bookmarked.
In the part of my life
Where you are still living.

—Sara Rain, Loving the gone

14
IT'S BACK

There have been a number of losses and traumatic events throughout my life. It never occurred to me that there had been so many. I suppose looking back over more than six decades of a full and richly lived life, it makes sense. I moved beyond each one with relative speed. Almost as if I needed to get the pain behind me as soon as I could. It's clear that efficiency around grief is not a productive goal. There is nothing efficient about grief. It will arise when one least expects it. A smell, a photograph, a memory—anyone of those can bring a wave of melancholy—a reminder of the hole in my heart that my mother or father filled.

If there is anything I believe I've done well, it is loving with all my heart. The human condition is such that loss is a regular occurrence—it is a common experience. Regardless of the fact that our culture skips over death in an effort to move on, each of us will grieve. Both the person suffering and those they encounter desire a return to normalcy as soon as possible. How that is done is an individual process and many times, we do it alone. Other than the funeral ritual, there is no formal period of mourning. We are expected to get on with life and leave our sadness behind. People are uncomfortable talking about death. One only has to replay what guests say at wakes and funerals to understand their great discomfort. Often, the mourners are left to comfort visitors who are at a loss not knowing what to say. It is not their fault. We don't have the language for grief.

The result is obvious. It's back to work or school—back to the daily grind as quickly as possible. While the rest of the world moves on, we are left with the weight of loss pressing on our hearts and minds. It sits with heaviness making it difficult to breathe, to move, to rise up and move on. The physical characteristics are as profound as the emotional. And yet, we are expected to put on brave faces, even smiles, and move forward with ordinary tasks. If we don't, people distance themselves from us or judge us. What is wrong with them? I thought they were stronger than that. Their depression is affecting their work. Our culture treats grief as a weakness, and that is to the detriment of us all. If we don't live our grief, and fully experience it, it will manifest itself in unhealthy and destructive ways.

Reflecting on the traumatic car accident I had over forty years ago, I feel great empathy for my twenty-year-old self. How did I survive such unimaginable pain? How did I process my grief? Keeping a journal was a significant vehicle toward mental health during my younger years. I wrote nearly every day for twenty years. To better understand how I processed my grief, I went back to read my journal entries from the months following the accident. The pages bleed with unreconciled pain. What strikes me is there is barely a month of writing about my feelings and how I tried to make sense of them, certainly not enough time to sort through the pain and trauma. My unimaginable suffering transformed into coping mechanisms to help me move on. Two months after my accident, I seemed to be on a similar path as my classmates—looking forward to commencement and a life beyond college. What springs off the pages of my journal is the realization that I never fully grieved, not enough. I didn't have the luxury of time nor the systematic support to process such profound trauma.

As a college senior, I had grand dreams for my life. Many of them were being realized. By my senior year of college, I held leadership roles in numerous clubs and activities at the university. I never dreamed I'd be respected, popular, and sought after. I had always dreamed of becoming a Catholic priest. From a very young age, I created an altar and said Mass. I dressed in vestments my mom sewed for me and placed my stuffed animals facing me. A dream come true, I was appointed to the most prestigious seminary in the Catholic stratosphere—the North American College in Vatican City. I was on top of the world and believed nothing could stop me. A bright and exciting future was already being realized. In the midst of that came death, and there was no space in my life to deal with it. I was crushed and I didn't have the capacity to process the pain. Its very occurrence was incongruous with all the wonderful aspects of my life at the time. My head was spinning, and my heart was broken. Nothing made sense to me. I didn't understand tragedy and death in the context of my perfect life.

I can still feel the chilly November air the day I exited the science building on campus and ran into Father McGrath. I can see his eyes, with laser focus, locked on mine. His grip on both my shoulders was so jarring. His gravelly voice echoes in my ears today.

"Don't you let anyone tell you that you should be over it! Not now, not ever. Do you hear me? You do this in your own time."

He literally shook me out of a self-destructive pattern of guilt. It was so jarring. It snapped me out of the need to please others, the belief that I shouldn't feel the pain, that I should quickly move on, and get on with life. Fr. McGrath gave me permission to grieve. But I didn't know how to do that. I wasn't offered the time or space to grieve. Life moved on at such a rapid pace that I never looked back. The next challenge or struggle was on the horizon. I could have taken a semester off, but I never permitted myself to do so.

At the same time, I was finally coming to terms with being a gay man in a church that viewed me as sinful. I recall the many times I knelt in Loyola Chapel wrestling with what I felt in my heart and mind, and what the church taught. Intertwined with my grief was the essential grappling with my identity and sexuality. I feared rejection from friends, family, and the Church I loved. Self-loathing compounded the guilt I bore over driving my car that night and killing a sixteen-year-old boy. These feelings became intricately intertwined—in some ways they were indistinguishable from each other.

My need to bond with someone on a romantic level was all-consuming. I desperately needed the human connection of being loved because I felt unlovable. There were so many narratives from various sources that told me I was unworthy, unhealthy, or sinful. I internalized that negativity. I believed they were true, which made me feel isolated and lonely. For many years, my psycho-emotional work centered around self-acceptance. It was the only way through my self-loathing and the only way to love.

Because of that, my grief was buried deep within. It is only after the death of my mother that it has resurfaced. What has come as a surprise to me, is the presence of a lifetime of unresolved grief. The loss of my dear mother has opened a floodgate of emotions. Moments of reflection flash numerous events from throughout my life that were never fully addressed. Each time I got knocked down, I rose to face another day with little consideration of the pain I experienced. I never let myself heal before getting back into the game.

Perhaps my defense mechanisms kicked into gear and gave me the strength to move on, to forge ahead. In fact, I am sure of it. I am grateful that I was able to function and continue my path forward. Not one of my losses or traumatic events completely broke me. There is great value in getting back on the horse after a fall. However, taking inventory after such a fall is just as important. And after assessing the damage, we must allow time for healing, just as we do for physical injuries. If I never address the hurt that was a result of the fall, how can I properly heal? If I had a broken leg, the doctor wouldn't tell me to work through the pain, to walk it off. We are all more comfortable with physical than emotional or psychological ailments. Our culture understands the need for a splint, cast, and crutches to heal properly. After the initial healing comes physical therapy to strengthen and increase the range of motion. That takes months.

Why don't we offer the same space for emotional injuries? Why is grief so different?

As I face my grief, there is a strange feeling of familiarity. I recognize it, and though it is painful, I welcome it into my heart once again. It has been the source of so much unfocused sadness throughout my life, calling out to me, demanding attention. Unresolved grief has been my companion for decades. It is now time to honor it and fully grieve.

Heaven knows we need never be ashamed of our tears,
for they are rain upon the blinding dust of earth,
overlying our hard hearts.
I was better after I had cried, than before – more sorry,
more aware of my own ingratitude,
more gentle.

—Charles Dickens, Great Expectations

15
AFTERLIFE?

My husband and I moved from New York to Sonoma County, California just over a year before Mom died. I still bear the guilt of leaving her in her final year. Two months before she passed, I flew back to Connecticut, missing the first week of school because she was in the hospital once again. My siblings and I worried that her time was at hand. We weren't sure she would leave the hospital alive. During that visit, Mom and I made a point of talking about everything, an opportunity for which I am so grateful. Neither of us wanted to leave anything unsaid. Feeling the physical distance between us weighed heavily on my heart. I asked if she felt I had abandoned her when we moved away. In her candor, she replied, "Yes, at first. But seeing how happy you are there brings me joy." Her words pierced my heart. It still aches from the truth she spoke. But Mom always spoke the truth.

When it came time for me to return to California, I didn't want to leave her. Just as I was getting ready to say goodbye, the visiting nurse came by. I looked on willing her to leave us alone. But she had to go through the paces of checking Mom's vitals. So, I put my arms around my mother, realizing that it was likely the last time I would see her. My composure was gone, and my body shook as I attempted to hold back my tears. Getting into the car, I sobbed the entire way to the airport.

I'm told that grief is a cross that may become lighter to bear with the passage of time. However, during those first weeks, the weight was suffocating.

On my visit nine months before, when Mom suffered from pneumonia, I looked forward to spending quality time with her. That January morning, we celebrated four winter birthdays, mine, my nephew, Matthew, my niece's husband, Charley, and my husband, Jim. The celebration lacked its usual festive atmosphere because Mom was absent from the table during dinner. She was weak, had trouble breathing, and needed the quiet of her room. The next day we brought her to the hospital.

It was a difficult week during which she prayed to be reunited with Dad. "Mario, I'm ready. I have lived a good life and it is time. I want to be with your father."

It pained me to hear her talk with such finality. But I could see that she was tired—tired of the struggle. She had been wearing that awful neck brace for nine months. She couldn't bear the prospect of wearing it for the rest of her life. Mom was miserable and wanted her suffering to end. I could see that. But what does it mean to be "ready?" I wonder what she believed would happen at that point. Did she envision her death? What might it have looked like to her? I am sure she thought only of the afterlife. In her heart, she could see herself holding hands with my father, spending time with the love of her life after thirteen years apart.

The vision of my parents, arm in arm, gives me comfort.

Given all I was taught about the afterlife or heaven, it is a scene that makes sense to me. But I am not convinced of its inevitability. Is that truly what happens when we die? Is there a great reunion of family and friends who have passed? I return to my original question. What does it mean to be ready? Did Mom understand death—the finality of it? The will to live is incredibly strong. I saw it just a few months later as my father-in-law continued to rebound from stroke, congestive heart failure, and kidney failure. His final days and weeks were spent curled up in a recliner, sleeping most of the day and night. He was ready, yet his body fought to live until it didn't. The mind, body, and soul fight to survive no matter what. What changes when a person says they are ready? Is there hope for a peaceful death? Or is it simply a desire to end one's suffering?

THE MEANING OF GRIEF

The demands of life do not allow time for grief. Life goes on whether or not one's heart is ready. As I've mentioned, most people don't know what to do with the grief of others. There is an unspoken desire to move beyond it—for the person in mourning to return to normal. Almost everyone I've encountered since my mother died seems uncomfortable addressing my grief. Some don't even acknowledge my loss. I have found that most difficult, at times offensive. It feels like a willful denial of what I am experiencing—a denial of my life at the moment. If one can't even say the obligatory, I'm sorry for your loss, how can we have an authentic conversation? I have said this before: our culture does not hold a space for grief. The brief rituals of a wake and funeral are over in a matter of days. Bereavement leave is almost nonexistent at most places of employment. Those who mourn are expected to comfort those who are uncomfortable with our grief, to let them off the hook when they don't know what to say. The burden is placed upon those who carry the weight of grief. We are expected to get on with life without the time to process the pain of loss.

Of course, I can function at work, teaching my wonderful high school students to sing and programming concerts. But when I come home at night, I am shrouded in loss. I often feel guilty about feeling grief over my mother. Everybody loses a parent and now both my parents are gone. I question the validity of my feelings. Why should I be feeling so much pain, so much loss? It pales in comparison to people who have lost a wife or husband or a child. A loss of that magnitude would be so much worse; and yet I still feel heaviness and pain.

At times, the pain is unbearable, like a throbbing deep in my chest. Yet, I fear its absence. Images of my father and my cousin, Frank come into focus—my memories of them have faded along with the pain of grief. It's almost as if time has allowed my memories to wither away. I don't love them any less, but the intensity of emotion that accompanied their passing has lessened. The lack of sadness is a blessing, but the lack of clarity in my memories is not. I don't want to lose that intensity concerning my mother. Somehow, it seems like a betrayal of my love for her. The realization that over time, memories fade along with one's grief leaves me cold. Will I forget the sound of their voices, the feel of their touch, or the look in their eyes? Is that the cost of my letting go of the pain of grief? I'm not sure that's a price I want to pay. As much as it hurts to remember my mother, knowing I can never sit with her, share a thought or a touch, the idea of forgetting moments together seems more painful.

The immediacy of grief allows me to rest in the love I have for my mother. With that comes the emptiness in my heart, the realization that she is gone. But in my thoughts, she is as present as she ever was. She lives in my heart and memories. I don't want to let that go. I suppose that is why we tell stories about our loved ones after they have died. We bring them back with images of laughter or tenderness. They live in our memories and in the present as we recall precious moments. Perhaps that is a glimpse of eternal life. They live on as we celebrate their memory.

Thanksgiving was just over a month after my mother died. It was always one of my favorite holidays. We always hosted my family and Mom joined my husband and me in the kitchen as we prepared the holiday feast. Instead, Jim and I drove out to the California coast to be alone. With so many questions swirling in my mind, I desperately needed to retreat from the busy schedule of life. The vastness of the Pacific Ocean called to me as my heart and mind were in great need of solace. I sought time away from the cacophony of high school students and my hectic schedule. When silence finally came, the finality of death lifted the cloak of protection. Standing naked in the sun, death burned through every fiber of my being as it tingled with the pain of loss.

By contrast, the grandeur of God splashed across the vast open sky as I sat watching the sunset over the Pacific Ocean, the craggy Sonoma coastline in the foreground. Images of the many trials I endured during my life came alive. With each one, I fought my way back to equanimity and contentedness. The lessons I learned, about myself and life in general are tangible. I emerged from each event with greater strength, more depth, and hopefully wisdom. But questions continue to invade my mind. What was the meaning of all my suffering? Why did that young man have to die? Why was it me driving the car during that fatal encounter? Was there truly a spiritual message bestowed upon me? Or was it simply another tragic accident in which there were no winners, just losers?

My faith life is so very different from that of my twenty-year-old self. Back then, I was devoutly Catholic. I was certain of the existence of God and the power of salvation through the death and resurrection of Jesus Christ. But after forty-five years of living, growing, suffering, and fully experiencing a life well-lived, I don't understand Christianity in the same way. Opening my bible to Isaiah the day after that awful accident brought me great comfort. In my darkest hour I read, "Do not be afraid, for I am with you." Those words came alive; they embraced me and held me in my despair. Was it the voice of God? Did he carry me when I could not walk on my own? Or was it simply a coincidence? Did I believe it because it was what I needed to hear?

At sixty-plus years of age, I continue to search for the meaning of life. In my seminary studies some forty years ago, this was a philosophical exercise. Now, it could not be more real. After the passing of both my parents, I question the purpose of life. Mom's bedroom was filled with photos and objects she collected over the years she spent on this earth. Each was valued and cherished for the memories they sparked. She was surrounded by precious moments from ninety-two years of a life well-lived. Those memories passed away with her. After her death, we dismantled the bedroom, and with it, her life. What did it all mean? My three siblings and I can never value those objects as she did, nor will we fully understand what they meant to her. I picture her fingering a set of wooden rosary beads from the Holy Land. I touch them almost every day longing to connect with her, to feel her presence once more. Mom lives on in our hearts and in our memories. But all that she experienced, her joys and her struggles, have ceased to exist. There is a finality to death like no other. Platitudes about heaven, living on in the presence of God, fall short. They are cold comfort when my heart is broken, and the pain of loss weighs heavily on both mind and body.

Reason tells me that life goes on, that the pain will lessen as time passes. That was certainly true for me after the tragic accident more than forty years ago. The first year was the most difficult, and for many years after, rainy October weather, fallen leaves, the scent of autumn, brought that pain right back to me. Images of that night came alive with vivid detail. October 24th was in my consciousness each year as summer turned to fall. But without my awareness, months and years passed, and I no longer thought of that dark night. My memories faded and the external cues failed to remind me of my pain. Indeed, time healed that wound.

But what of my search for meaning? Did God or Jesus speak to me through the scriptures? Did I truly feel the warmth of God's arms wrapped around my shaking body? I honestly don't know. I recall people telling me, "Everything happens for a reason," or saying, "We can never know God's plan for us." To this day, I bristle at those phrases. What kind of God purposely inflicts pain on people to teach them lessons? How cruel a creator that would be. A parent would be charged with child abuse if they allowed injury or harm to hurt their children in an attempt to teach them a lesson. Why would we expect God to be any different?

But somehow, we do. This is not unique to one brand of Christianity. I hear this from Catholics, Episcopalians, and Evangelicals. The image of God from each institutional church is conflated. Most devout Catholics or Episcopalians don't know the difference between their official teaching of free will, a God who doesn't interfere with the workings of the world, and the belief of predestination that many other churches espouse.

But it is an essential difference. If God grants us free will, any interference in our lives would take that away. If God has a plan for us or places trials in our lives, He is interfering with our free will.

Ultimately, I believe that it is up to the individual to draw meaning from life's events. We choose how to respond to the trials in life. Some of us remain broken for much longer than others. Each of us approaches life with the tools we are equipped with. So how does God factor into the equation?

Elusive Light 141

When our days become dreary
with low-hovering clouds of despair,
and when our nights become darker
than a thousand midnights,
let us remember that there is a creative force in this
universe, working to pull down
the gigantic mountains of evil,
a power that is able to make a way out
of no way and transform dark yesterdays into
bright tomorrows.

—Martin Luther King, Jr.

16
GOD

How can I possibly tackle the question of God when centuries of philosophers and theologians have come up short? Does God exist? Is God an anthropomorphic being after whose image we are created? Does God play an active role in our human lives, directing and aiding us in times of need? Or did God create the world like a great clockmaker only to set it in motion while She stands back to observe? These are not new questions. But they are lasting ones. Hundreds have written about God and the role She plays in the world.

What of evil? How do we make sense of the presence of evil in the world? How does God factor into the willful destruction propagated by world leaders? Then there is the question of how God factors into the occurrence of natural disasters or tragic accidents. Many use their mere existence as proof that God does not exist. For me, that is too simple. The human condition is complex. Our lives seem to be a constant search for meaning. We seek to understand the universe through science and philosophy. So many books have been written about the meaning of suffering in the world. None have come to any ground-breaking conclusions. Perhaps that is because there isn't a definitive conclusion.

I am left with my initial reflections regarding pain and suffering. It seems clear to me that I have a choice. I am the only one responsible for my response to suffering. I can let it crush me—crumbling under the weight of my pain. Or I can choose life. I can dust myself off and stumble through until I regain my strength. The truth is that unless I fully experience the pain of grief and loss, I will continue to bumble through my life. Ignoring the weight of grief may allow me to succeed in life's endeavors, but unless I allow it to surface, that load will continue to hold me under the surface of the waters of life. I imagine myself gasping for air, my face breaking the surface of the vast ocean, just as I did on that harrowing sailing trip. The weight of my grief pulls my body and mind downward. If I don't let it out, I may drown under its weight.

Since I was a child, I feared the open ocean. The vast, gray expanse of water with its never-ending waves overwhelms me. I recall the feeling in the pit of my stomach when the depth meter on the sailboat could not measure any longer. We had sailed beyond its capacity—the waters were thousands of feet deep. The great force of the ocean terrified me. Nothing I could do would matter if it raged against me. I was but a drop in the vastness of the ocean. Perhaps the ocean is a metaphor for God. Do I quake before the image of God? I know that I could do nothing to prevent the suffering I have experienced throughout my life. Death is a necessary part of living. Our loved ones will die. Accidents happen. We continue to make poor choices and bear the consequences. That is living.

Just as I did in the middle of the Atlantic Ocean, I am reading the depth meter of life. I had two choices on the deck of that boat. I could demand that we turn back, and head to the safety of the shore. Or I could face my fear and forge ahead come what may. If I am sailing the open ocean of life, I don't really have a choice. There isn't a safe harbor at the shore to which I can turn. If I choose not to surf the waters of life, then I am choosing not to live. The question remains: Is God the ocean? Do I tremble in fear because of Her greatness?

I don't know the answer to that question. The simpler faith of my childhood has long faded. I don't believe that God guides us and keeps us from harm. The harm I have experienced throughout my life has taught me that. But I don't blame a white-bearded old man in the sky for all the ills of life. That doesn't make sense to me. It's too simple or perhaps childish.

I suppose I believe in the supernatural—in something greater than myself. But I am not clear on what form it takes. Perhaps it is energy in the vast universe, or a great assembly of the souls who have passed before us. The Gnostics believe there is a divine spark in each of us. If that is the case, God is ablaze in the communion of humanity. That is an image that resonates with me. Connecting with people during the process of grieving eliminates the isolation—the icy chill of loneliness. Perhaps it is there where I discover the elusive light I've been searching for. Could that spark of the divine be the flame that melts the ice of grief?

Pondering the meaning of life in the face of death has prompted me to question all that I have ever believed. It's an exercise that rocks my foundation. In some ways, it feels as if I am starting anew, building a new spiritual home. If there is one thing of which I am sure, it's that I am uncertain. I don't know what form my belief system will take or if it will be definable. Perhaps it is meant to evolve as it has throughout my life. It is less comfortable to live with ambiguity. I prefer clean definitions—clear rules of engagement. My journey defies my desire for certitude.

I continue to hope I will hear my mother's voice or feel her touch, whether that be in my dreams or when taking a walk along the shore. When I am alone with my thoughts, I hope to chat with her as I did with Dad after he died. It may be that I'm not ready to feel the depth of pain from her death. Until I am, I continue to make her tomato sauce and meatballs. I will bake her favorite taralli, (Italian pretzels) fry zucchini patties, and try to find her in the ordinary traditions we coveted.

In a culture that doesn't hold a place for those who mourn, I must give myself permission to do so whenever the ache of grief surfaces. I will allow the sadness to enter my heart without pushing it back down. For when I feel that pain, I am remembering the great love I shared with Mom, Dad, and Frank. In letting the memories of my traumatic accidents surface, I allow myself to be compassionate to my younger self. I can be kind to myself when I am hurting rather than berate myself for feeling hurt or believing I am weak. I have begun to communicate my feelings to my co-workers and friends rather than keeping them inside and further isolating myself in grief. When asked how I am feeling, I respond honestly. "I am feeling low today. I am missing Mom." The conversation shifts into truth, then I go on with my day. I don't give anyone time to feel uncomfortable while they search for the right words to say in response. Letting people know what is in my heart honors those feelings. But it also lets those I work with or love into my space. It gives them permission to be with me in my grief without the expectation of a response or finding the words to make me feel better. They don't have the power to take away my pain or lift me from my grief. I don't want them to do so. It is mine. My grief manifests itself because of my love for those I lost.

Something else has changed in me since my mother died. Perhaps it is not simply due to the grief over her loss alone. These days, weeks, and months of reflection have prompted a significant amount of psychic work. Processing decades of loss, searching for comfort in each and perhaps an over-arching meaning, I realize that I have given myself permission to say no. I have always felt the burden of responsibility, of being bound to duty. My need to please others was often destructive, damaging my own mental health.

Since I was a child, I have sought to do what is right and what was expected of me. I sought to be the good Catholic boy who puts others before himself. I volunteer to take on more work or serve when there is a need—often to my own detriment. But that is what the Scriptures taught. And so, the weight of my commitments lay heavily upon my shoulders. My identity is tightly woven into the fabric of selflessness—giving of time and effort to others until it hurts. This is too great a burden for me to carry any longer.

It may be that the words my mother spoke to me after her pneumonia have begun to sink in. She truly believed it would be the last time she would see me, and she was determined to leave me with a final admonition.

"Mario, just remember that you are good just the way you are. I love you with all my heart and you are loved deeply by so many others. Know that you are kind and loving. You must believe in yourself."

I stopped her as she spoke. I didn't want to believe that she was saying goodbye. Although I know she was, I wasn't ready. Reflecting on her words, the message has come into focus. I don't have to work so hard to prove my worth. I don't have to give so much of myself to others such that I have nothing left for myself. Mom told me to take better care of myself, to love myself, and know my value. It's long past time to let go of the image of the suffering servant. I need to cease drawing from an empty well so that I can refill, recharge, and live a healthy life.

This realization did not appear one day as a bright light. It has been a gradual change in my perception. During the early days of my grieving, I turned down invitations to gatherings. I let go of commitments at church and work. In my sadness, I allowed myself to back away from things I believed I "should" have been doing. Gradually, I began to feel stronger about choosing events or commitments that nourished me rather than those that depleted me. I felt a great sense of freedom from how others perceived me or my actions.

Perhaps that is an unforeseen gift of my grief—the freedom to say no to anything that doesn't nourish me. Strangely, I don't feel guilt at turning down gatherings or letting go of commitments I've made out of a sense of duty. There is more to living than doing what is expected of us. After all these years on earth, I understand that I can choose myself and those I love. That last statement sounds so unchristian, however, it also feels like a healthier path toward self-fulfillment.

•••

So where do we go from here? How do we find light amidst the darkness? For many years, it seemed just beyond my reach. However, if I rest in my grief, and allow myself to feel the weight of my loss, I will also be spending time with those whom I love. For me, connecting with others in my grief allows me to see the light. Perhaps it is the spark of the divine in each of us that will set my heart ablaze with love.

I'm still waiting for the sparks to catch fire, to brighten my spirit. I see glimpses of light, moments of happiness, and even joy in my daily life. It still hurts when photos of Mom pop up on social media. My heart aches when I realize she is gone. I know there will come a time when I will tell stories about her and laugh. It happened after my father died. It will happen for Mom as well.

Something different has happened since she died. My intense relationship with her prompted me to reflect on my life. Throughout these pages, I revisited some of the most painful events I've ever experienced. Reliving them has been torturous at times. But it has also given me new insights into who I am and where I have come from. Throughout this journey, I have come to understand myself better. By letting myself experience grief, I have experienced compassion, sympathy, and love. These don't simply remain in my heart. No, they can't help but pour out of me into everything I do, and toward everyone I love. Grief has allowed me to more intimately connect with and relate to others on a deeper level. I have less tolerance for the superficial.

Nothing will ever take away the empty place that death leaves. Those are sacred rooms where I hold vigil for those I loved and lost. I don't want someone to fill that space. No one ever can. Through this process, I discovered I can return to those sacred rooms to visit, to mourn, to love them. Meanwhile, my life goes on and I am forever changed by each occurrence and each form of grief. Perhaps the elusive light I seek has been with me all along—in each relationship, in each loss, in the divine sparks I encounter every day. That light takes on a different hue just as it does at different times in the day—brilliantly clear in the morning, high and bright at noon, golden in the late afternoon. Colors change with the light as it casts shadows or turns the ordinary into amber flames glowing with love. Landscapes come alive or fade into the light depending on the time of day just as my grief transforms or reveals itself in a new or unexpected way. I am confident in the knowledge that grief is not something to be avoided or ignored. It is part of life because death is a part of life. In defiance of our grief-denying culture, I embrace grief in order to embrace life. Perhaps that is how elusive light shines most brightly.

Acknowledgments

When I began writing this book, I was not clear of the outcome. Was my writing an exercise in journaling? Was I working through my emotions, my grief? As the months passed and I continued to write, I witnessed a body of work taking shape. Still, I was not sure what the end result would be. So, I turned to authors I respect and admire; I sought their counsel asking them an essential question. What should I do with these pages?

I thank each of them for contributing to my reflections on grief. Halo Scot, you have always been a champion of mine, spurring me on to write more, giving wings to my thoughts and accuracy to my words. Claudia Oltean, your journalistic sensibilities challenged me to focus on what it was I wanted to say. You led me to dig deeper.

Matt Speiser, I anticipate your feedback with great excitement. You never let me doubt my abilities. Your faith in my voice and the ability to bring it to life has made me a better writer. I am so grateful to have such a brilliant writing companion and dear friend.

To Anne Gardner, over forty years of friendship gave you a profound understanding of my journey. You listened and asked leading questions prompting me to refine my thoughts and define my purpose in writing. You have more insight into my journey of grief than most. Thank you for being at my side.

To my siblings, Annette, Franco, and Maria, we began this journey of grief together. Each of us responding in our unique ways. Thank you for being my wise big sisters and brother, and for allowing me to take this journey with you.

Finally, to my dear husband, we both lost our last living parents within months of each other. Although we approach our grief in drastically different ways, you have never left my side, never expected me to be anything but myself. We travel this road together, as we have always done.

Dr. Mario Dell'Olio is a 2022 winner of the Premio Vincenzo Crocitti International award for literature and music. He is the author of several books: Letters from Italy is the love story of his immigrant parents, which is also published in Italian, Lettere Dall'Italia. A memoir, Coming About: Life in the Balance, is about a sailing adventure going terribly wrong. Tilting Toward the Sun, Body And Soul, and Forbidden Rome, LGBTQA+ fiction that explore the strife of coming out during the 1980s.

He is the music director at Sonoma Academy, an independent school in Sonoma County, California. Previously, he was chair of the music department and ethics teacher at Marymount School of New York, a school for girls in Manhattan. Dr. Mario Dell'Olio conducted the Concert and Chamber

Choirs. He has led his choirs on international and domestic concert tours and released numerous albums on iTunes and Amazon.com. Dr. Dell'Olio was director of music at Mission Dolores Basilica in San Francisco, California, from 1990 to 2000. He led the Basilica Choir's first international concert tour to Italy in June 1999. Dr. Dell'Olio holds a Doctor of Sacred Music, a Master of Music in Vocal Performance, and a Master of Religious Education. He pursued postgraduate work in Theology at the Pontifical Gregorian University, Rome, Italy.

With over 35,000 followers on X and a solid social media presence, he actively participates in the Writing Community. Dr. Dell'Olio has scheduled numerous author events, readings, and book signings. In November 2020, The Empire City Men's Chorus of New York City performed a concert/documentary based on Dell'Olio's book, Coming About.

https://mariodellolio.com

NOTE FROM THE AUTHOR

Word-of-mouth is crucial for any author to succeed. If you enjoyed Elusive Light, please leave a review online—anywhere you are able. Even if it's just a sentence or two. It would make all the difference and would be very much appreciated.

Thank You!

Mario Dell'Olio

Begining Chapter Image by Gordon Johnson from Pixabay

Heart Image by ViolkaArt from Pixabay

Other images from Pixabay

Also by Mario Dell'Olio

Letters from Italy: A Transatlantic Love Story

Tilting Toward the Sun: A Chance to Love

Coming About: Life In the Balance

Body and Soul

Forbidden Rome

www.ingramcontent.com/pod-product-compliance
Lightning Source LLC
Chambersburg PA
CBHW072201070526
44585CB00015B/1239